# PRONUNCIATION EXERCISES
# for ESL

## (Advanced Level)

Gary Esarey

Ann Arbor

## THE UNIVERSITY OF MICHIGAN PRESS

First published by the University of Michigan Press 1990
Copyright © 1977, University of Pittsburgh Press and the
  English Language Institute, University of Pittsburgh
All rights reserved
ISBN 0-472-08112-8
Published in the United States of America by
The University of Michigan Press
Manufactured in the United States of America

1995  1994                    5  4

# CONTENTS

# Preface

Gary Esarey wrote *Pronunciation Exercises for Advanced Learners of English as a Second Language* while he was teaching at the English Language Institute. Upon receiving his M.A. degree in linguistics, he took a position at Nanyang University in Singapore. The time-consuming and laborious task of revising the two preliminary versions in light of classroom usage in the Institute subsequently fell on Patricia Furey and Mary Newton Bruder. In Gary Esarey's absence, I take it upon myself to acknowledge that without the unstinting editorial assistance of Patricia Furey and Mary Bruder this text would not exist in its present shape and to thank them, as Gary would want me to do, for that help. Thanks are also due to the many classroom teachers in the Institute who used the text and whose many comments and suggestions contributed to its improvement. Mary Bruder deserves further thanks for seeing the text through the stages of publication, reading page proofs and all the rest.

Christina Bratt Paulston
Director
English Language Institute

v

# Introduction to the Teacher

This text is designed for intermediate and advanced (TOEFL 450+) students of English as a second or foreign language, who have mastered the basic sound system of English but who still need to practice the more "difficult" sounds and complex stress and intonation patterns. The segments and patterns were chosen on the basis of an error analysis of the speech of intermediate and advanced students of many language backgrounds at the English Language Institute, University of Pittsburgh.

## Procedures for Use

The text is designed for use in conjunction with other materials and is not intended to be a primary classroom text. In the English Language Institute teachers spend from 5-10 minutes per class session on these materials, and complete a lesson, on the average, every two days. In general all exercises are done with books open.

### I. Recognition and Production

This section has lists of minimal pairs containing the target sounds for the lesson. The students are to do three things: listen, discriminate between (or among) the sounds, and produce the sounds correctly.

The teacher writes a minimal pair of words containing the target sounds on the board and labels them #1 and #2 respectively. When the teacher says a word containing sound #1, the students raise one hand; sound #2, they raise two hands. This technique permits the teacher to see quickly if the students have any problem with the distinction. As soon as the students can discriminate between the sounds, they move to the production stage, repeating the pairs of sounds after the teacher. Directions for the exercise precede each one or are included in the heading. E.g. Repetition, Read and Look up. (The student reads the sentence to himself and then looks up and says it without referring to the printed page.) Students who have special difficulty with individual sounds can be assigned extra practice in the language laboratory.

### II. and III. Stress and Intonation

There are several types of exercises in this section. The teacher should read the directions for each ahead of the class. The stress and intonation marks are provided for teacher modeling, which should be practiced aloud ahead of class, but not overly prepared. It is important to provide models of normal intonation and stress.

Generalizations and rules precede the exercises which exemplify them. The students may not always need the generalization before the exercise, but a brief classroom discussion about language is often profitable at this level of proficiency.

Many of the exercises in these sections require the students to mark the stress and intonation in their books. Sometimes the teacher provides a model before the students write; in others the students write without a model. The students then take turns producing their answers.

## Cumulative Dialogs

The dialogs are designed to present a context for the major points of the lesson and to give the students the opportunity of identifying the major affective patterns of English intonation such as anger, joy etc. The same characters recur throughout the dialogs, in a continuing saga of students trying to make their way through graduate school in an American university.

Memorization of the dialogs is not encouraged. The lines are purposely long in order to give practice putting together phrases and clauses in the way native speakers do.

If the accompanying tapes are used, little class time need be spent on reading the dialogs. The students listen ahead of time in the laboratory and class time is spent on identification and the use of the various stress and intonation patterns.

In the later lessons, there are a number of questions designed to elicit discussion about 1) certain characteristics of spoken English as revealed in the dialogs and 2) the content of the dialogs. The teacher should point out (or have the students identify) characteristics of the various styles of speech including phonology, syntax and lexical items.

*Vocabulary*

The students should be responsible for looking up ahead of class unfamiliar vocabulary, both in the exercises and in the dialogs. Little class time should be spent except in clarifying idiomatic expressions not likely to be found in dictionaries.

*Homework*

Written exercises are provided at the end of each lesson. They can be turned in and corrected by the teacher or corrected orally in class depending upon the classroom situation.

*A Word of Thanks*

Finally, I would like to acknowledge my debt to Christina Bratt Paulston for her help in the design and preparation of the original work and to Mary Newton Bruder for input and help on the first revision.

Gary Esarey
English Language Institute—Pitt
June 1977

# LESSON ONE — The /θ/ Sound —

## I Recognition and Production

— Repetition —

| /θ/ | /t/ | | /θ/ | /s/ |
|-----|-----|---|-----|-----|
| thank | tank | | thick | sick |
| thin | tin | | thought | sought |
| thick | tick | | worth | worse |
| three | tree | | mouth | mouse |

| /θ/ | /t/ | /s/ |
|-----|-----|-----|
| thin | tin | sin |
| thick | tick | sick |
| thought | taught | sought |
| path | pat | pass |
| tenth | tent | tense |

## II Stress

— Repetition —

thánks a lót      twó or thrée
wórth a fórtune      Míster Smíth
through thíck and thín      on the ténth of the mónth
Ópen your móuth please.
Brúsh your téeth thrée tímes a dáy.
Bóth Tím and Béth are síck.
Mr. Smíth sáid he'd thínk it óver.
She táught us to thínk for oursélves.

## III Intonation (Falling)

*Generalization:* At the end of many English sentences the pitch tends to fall sharply. Ordinary statements and Wh-questions (*Who, What, When, Where, Why, How much, How many,* etc.) are usually spoken with falling intonation.

1   —  Questions and Answers: Repetition   —

| Question | Answer |
|---|---|

1. What did you think of the te͞st?            I thought it was ea\sy.
2. When did you thank\ him?                    I thanked him before I le\ft.
3. What's wrong with the cloth?                I think it's too thick.
4. How much is it worth?                       It's not worth a thing.
5. How often do you take a bath?               At least three times a month.

2   —  Interview   —

One student in the class is interviewed by the others. The others should ask Wh-questions to gain biographical information.

Example questions:

| S1 | How old are you? | S2 | (I'm 24 years old.) |
|---|---|---|---|
| S3 | How many brothers and sisters do you have? | S2 | (I have two brothers and a sister.) |
| S4 | How long have you been in the USA? | S2 | (I've been here for six months now.) |
| | etc. | | |

3   —  Dialog   —

Listen to the following dialog.

Health Insurance

Clerk:  What's your address, Sir?

Richard:  4627 North Ellis Street. That's here in town.

Clerk:  That's a nice neighborhood. How do you like it?

Richard:  The neighborhood is fine, but we don't like the rent very much.

5     Clerk:  Who does! Just a few more questions, Mr. Crosby. How many people will be included in the coverage?

Richard:  Just me and my wife. What do we do when we want to renew it next year?

Clerk:  Just stop by here again next year and let us know. For details on your coverage you can look through our brochure. The policy includes major hospital expenses and doctors'

10     fees for both you and your wife. By the way, Sir, I need your I.D. number. And the name of your department.

Richard:  Well, I'm afraid I don't have one yet.

Clerk:  Don't have what?

Richard:  A department. You see, I haven't . . . uh . . . decided yet what department will

15     accept me.

Clerk:  I see. Then, what is your status? You have to be a registered student to get health insurance.

Richard:  Well, I'm almost registered. I'm sure it's just a matter of two or three days now.

Clerk:  Mr. Crosby, I think you'd better wait a couple of days until you get registered.

20     Then come back and complete your application.

Richard:  But what if I get sick today?

Clerk:  I'm afraid there's nothing we can do now. Here. Take a couple of aspirin and hope for the best.

## LESSON TWO — Voiced / Voiceless Sounds —

**I Recognition and Production**

1 — The /ð/ Sound: Repetition —

| | | |
|---|---|---|
| then | this | father |
| they | that | mother |
| those | these | bathe |
| the | brother | breathe |

*Note:* The /ð/ sound above is not the same as the /θ/ sound practiced in Lesson One. The /ð/ sound is voiced; that is, it is produced when the vocal cords are vibrating. The sound in Lesson One is voiceless; the vocal cords do not vibrate.

2 — Voiced / Voiceless Contrasts: Repetition —

| Voiced /ð/ | Voiceless /θ/ |
|---|---|
| either | ether |
| teethe | teeth |
| wreathe | wreath |
| sheathe | sheath |

*Note:* The sounds /z/ and /s/ show a similar contrast. /z/ is voiced and /s/ is voiceless.

| /z/ | /s/ |
|---|---|
| zoo | Sue |
| zone | sewn |
| seizing | ceasing |
| razor | racer |
| lazy | lacy |
| plays | place |
| eyes | ice |
| buzz | bus |

3

## II   Stress

—   Words in Phrases: Repetition   —

that's that                              thanks a lot
both of them                             worth a fortune
then and there                           either of them
lazy summer days                         this, that and the other
            Face the facts, Smith.
            Close your eyes please.
            It's a nice place to visit.
            Please speak slowly.
            Both of them are thinking it over.

## III   Intonation

1   —   Review of Falling Intonation: Repetition   —

| Question | Answer |
|---|---|
| 1. Who's that? | That's my brother. |
| 2. How often does your mother call? | She calls every other day. |
| 3. How's the weather outside? | It's still snowing. |
| 4. Why didn't she sign the lease? | She says the house is just a mess. |

2   —   Gathering Information   —

The class divides into two groups. Each group selects one student to be interviewed by the others. The other students should ask Wh-questions to gather the items of information listed below. The group which first gathers the data *accurately,* wins.

Examples:

| Interviewers (take turns asking questions) | | Interviewee (may not look at book) | |
|---|---|---|---|
| S1 | How long have you lived here? | S2 | I've lived here for three months. |
| S3 | What's your major field? | S2 | I'm a chemist. |
| S4 | What kind of visa do you have? | S2 | A student visa. |

Information to be gathered:

1. Name
2. Age
3. Address
4. Place of birth
5. Date of birth
6. Marital status
7. Hometown
8. Home country

9. Height and weight
10. Shoe size
11. Favorite (American) food
12. Years of English studied
13. Year of high school graduation
14. Number of foreign countries visited
15. Distance between here and your own country

## LESSON THREE  —  Rhythm  —

### I  Recognition and Production

— The /v/ and /f/ Sounds: Repetition

| | | | | | |
|---|---|---|---|---|---|
| van | fan | rival | rifle | save | safe |
| vat | fat | reviews | refuse | live (adj.) | life |
| view | few | saver | safer | thieve | thief |
| vine | fine | invest | infest | believe | belief |

---

*Note:* The /v/ and /f/ sounds have the same contrast as the sounds in Lesson Two. /v/ is voiced and /f/ is voiceless.

---

### II  Rhythm

1  — Words in Phrases: Repetition  —

a safe investment
awfully valuable
a close shave
a beautiful view

a perfect fit
a lovely face
bitter rivals
a revolution in values

What a relief!
Save your breath.
You'd better refuse the offer.
I don't feel like saving money.

---

*Generalization:*  Rhythm is the alternation of stressed and unstressed syllables. Stressed syllables are louder, more distinct, and easier to hear. Certain kinds of words *tend to be* stressed and other kinds tend to be unstressed.

| Stressed Words | Unstressed Words |
|---|---|
| nouns | articles (*a/an, the*) |
| main verbs | prepositions |
| adjectives | pronouns |
| adverbs | conjunctions (*and, or, but*) |
| demonstratives (*that, this, those, these*) | |
| negatives (*not*) | |

---

5

2 — Identification —

Listen to the following sentences and mark the stressed syllables.

Example:

They refúsed to sígn the léase.

1. Sing a song.
2. That's a stupid question.
3. You're driving me crazy.

4. They've found an easy answer.
5. Please pass me the toast.
6. How's the weather in Pittsburgh?

## III  Intonation

1 — Review of Falling Intonation: Repetition —

| Question | Answer |
|---|---|
| Who's living there n⌐ow? | No⌐body. The place is va⌐cant. |
| How fast can you drive⌐ it? | Only about 40 miles an ho⌐ur. |
| Why did she refuse the offer? | She said they didn't offer enough benefits. |
| How often do you visit New York? | I almost never go there. |

2 — Question and Answer —

Examples:

where / good restaurant

S1  Where is a good restaurant in (Oakland)?
S2  (I don't think there is one.)

how often / have concerts

S2  How often do they have concerts here?
S3  (At least once a week.)

when / baseball season begin
what / best movie theater in town
where / cheap entertainment
how much / cost to (see a movie)
where / go (for a picnic)
when / beginning of the football season
where / see (basketball) games
who / sponsors concerts
where / get information on university clubs
where / buy tickets for the (opera)
where / go to get a (driver's license)
how / rent a car

3  —  Homework  —

Read the following sentences. Write in the stress marks and intonation lines. Remember that there is *no absolutely certain or correct* way to mark stress in English. Not everybody will say the same words in the same way. If possible, ask a native speaker to say these sentences. Be prepared to say them yourself in class.

Example:

She invested her money in the safest stocks she could find.

1. He answered a few of our questions.
2. Fred and Bev are building a house in the suburbs.
3. Whose books fell on the floor?
4. He takes no interest in saving money.
5. How many letters did you send to your family?
6. Phil and his brother refused to follow their father's advice.
7. Who's the ugliest man in your neighborhood?
8. He went to the office to work on his thesis.
9. How far do you travel to school?
10. Alice eats fried grits and lettuce for breakfast every morning.

---

*Note:* If the last word of the sentence is stressed, the intonation falls on the vowel of that word.
  Example:

    She said she didn't mind.

  If the last word is unstressed, the intonation falls before the unstressed word.
  Example:

    She said she didn't mind it.

## LESSON FOUR — Rising Intonation —

### I Recognition and Production

— The /b/ and /v/ Sounds: Repetition —

| boat | vote | ribbon | riven | robe | rove |
|------|------|--------|-------|------|------|
| buy | vie | marble | marvel | curb | curve |
| best | vest | cupboard | covered | dub | dove |
| bolt | volt | cabs | calves | jibe | jive |
| ban | van | curbing | curving | swab | suave |

### II Stress

1 — Words in Phrases: Repetition —

| | |
|---|---|
| bán the bómb | búy the véry bést |
| lét the búyer bewáre | gíve a vét a jób |
| cúrb your dóg | bánned in Bóston |
| twélve loáves of bréad | búy tíckets in advánce |

2 — Identification —
Listen to the following sentences and mark the stressed words.
  Example:
    He néver wéars a belt.

1. Bev's got bats in her belfry.
2. Buyers have to beware of bargains.
3. He always buys the very best beer.
4. You don't have to have a lot of money.
5. Baseball fans never fail to buy tickets well in advance.

3 — Identification —
Read the following sentences and mark the stressed words. The teacher will *not* read them aloud until after you have finished.
  Example:
    Leáve your dóg at hóme.

1. Give it to him on his birthday.
2. The beans are cooking on the stove.

this exercise continued on next page

3. He was playing basketball and broke his rib.
4. Bob covered the bench with a blanket.
5. I'll never vote for that corrupt bum again!

## III   Rising Intonation

*Generalization:* Rising intonation usually occurs at the end of Yes / No questions, such as:

Are you go/ing?
Do you have/time?

The answers to such questions usually carry falling intonation:

| | |
|---|---|
| Are you go/ing? | Yes, I a\m. |
| Do you have/time? | Yes, I do. |

Notice, however, that any sentence, phrase, or word may become a question if rising intonation is applied, as in these examples:

You're going/now?
So / soon?
Re/ally?

### 1  —  Repetition  —

| Question | Answer |
|---|---|
| 1. Are you feeling any better/today? | No, I'm afraid no\t. |
| 2. You're leaving without / me? | You can't go if you have the fl\u. |
| 3. Is today Friday the seventeenth? | No, I think it's Thursday. |
| 4. Are you going to miss another day of class? | Well, it doesn't really matter. |

### 2  —  Recognition  —

If you hear a *Question* (rising intonation), answer "I don't know."
If you hear a *Statement* (falling intonation), answer "Oh, that's too bad."

Example:

| T | | S | |
|---|---|---|---|
| | Is he going with / us? | | I don't know. |
| | He's leaving /now? | | I don't know. |
| | I'm not feeling \well. | | Oh, that's too bad. |

It's raining outside.
He's leaving town.
Is today Friday the seventeenth?
She's not coming today?
The bus drivers are on strike.
Has he left on his vacation?
He got a traffic ticket?
Victor forgot to open a savings
    account.
None of them remembered to
    bring their books?

3  —  Guess the Identity  —
One student is a famous person, someone known to all (Lenin, Napoleon, George
Washington, etc.). The other students guess his identity by asking Yes / No questions.
Questions should be answered only with *yes* or *no*.
   Example:

|        |                           |      |        |
|--------|---------------------------|------|--------|
| S1     | Are you a politician?     | A2   | Yes.   |
| S2     | Do you live in the country? | A3 | No.    |

4  —  Dialog  —
Listen to the following dialog. Be prepared to identify the intonation patterns you hear.

### A Case of the Flu

Richard: Are you feeling any better today? Well enough to get out of bed?
Arnold: I'm afraid not. I'll have to miss another day of class. I've got this cough and
    an awful sore throat.
Richard: Sounds like the flu. Too bad you can't join us. You should never get the
5    flu on Fridays.
Arnold: Friday? Friday the seventeenth? You mean this is the day we leave for
    Niagara Falls?
Richard: I'm sorry you feel so lousy. We'll send you a postcard.
Arnold: You're going to leave without me?
10   Richard: You can't get out of bed. Remember?
Arnold: What do you mean I can't get out of bed? A little fresh air is just what I
    need. Save me a seat on the bus.

Questions

1. What questions have rising intonation? Circle them.
2. Line 11. What intonation does the first sentence have? Is this really a
   question?

# LESSON FIVE — Stress and Intonation —

## I  Recognition and Production

— Review of Voiced / Voiceless Contrasts: Repetition —

| Voiced | Voiceless | | Voiced | Voiceless |
|--------|-----------|---|--------|-----------|
| believe | belief | | zoo | Sue |
| save | safe | | lazy | lacy |
| van | fan | | eyes | ice |
| vine | fine | | phase | face |
| invest | infest | | either | ether |

## II  Stress

1 — Words in Phrases: Repetition —

bánned in Bóston

lázy súmmer dáys

through thíck and thín

áwfully váluable

twélve loáves of bréad

a níce pláce to vísit

thén and thére

a béautiful víew

You have to fáce the fácts.

We bóught tíckets in advánce.

I néver feel lázy on Frídays.

Bóth his brothers are thoúghtless búms.

2 — Identification —

Listen to the following sentences and mark the stress.

Example:

Dón't bóther to búy tíckets in advánce.

1. Both boys were afraid of their fathers.
2. Very few athletes are professionals.
3. They selected two or three dozen pieces of toast for breakfast.
4. The weather in this place can easily drive you crazy.
5. Three or four bottles of gin are quite enough for a party.

3 — Identification —

Read the following sentences and mark stress. The teacher will *not* read them aloud until after you have finished.

Example:

We thóught it was wórth a fórtune.

1. Both of the boys got sick at the dance.
2. Try to hold your breath for three or four minutes.
3. The best place to buy a vest is at a clothing store.
4. Bus fares were increased to fifty cents a ride.
5. She's sick of reading bad reviews of the movies she likes best.

## III  Intonation

— Question and Answer Game "How Do You Feel?" —

One student is given the answer to a simple question, such as "How do you feel?"
Suppose S1 is given the answer "sleepy" by the teacher. The other students must
then ask Yes / No questions to determine the correct answer. Each question should
be limited to *one word*—made a question by rising intonation only.

Example game:

|  |  |  |  |
|---|---|---|---|
| "How do you feel?" | | S1 | ("sleepy") |
| Ss:  Ti/red? | | S1 | No. |
| Hungry? | | | No. |
| Unhappy? | | | No. |
| Broke? | | | No. |
| etc. | | | |
| Sleepy? | | | Yes. |

Suggested questions and possible answers

| "How do you feel?" | (sleepy, exhausted, excited, nervous, embarrassed) |
|---|---|
| "What kind of person are you?" | (kind, lazy, intelligent, rich) |
| "What's your favorite food?" | (pizza, curry, hamburgers, ice cream) |
| "What are you thinking of?" | (money, women, vacation, home, lunch) |
| "Where would you like to live?" | (Pittsburgh, Tokyo, Saudi Arabia, Paris, Sao Paulo) |

# LESSON SIX — Voiced / Voiceless Changes —

## I  Recognition and Production

> *Generalization:* In some words consonants change from voiceless to *voiced* when the words are used as verbs.

### 1 — Repetition —

| *Voiceless* (Adjective) | *Voiced* (Verb) |
|---|---|
| close | close |
| loose | lose |
| safe | save |
| loath | loathe |

| (Noun) | (Verb) |
|---|---|
| teeth | teethe |
| strife | strive |
| belief | believe |
| proof | prove |
| excuse | excuse |
| breath | breathe |
| grief | grieve |
| half | halve |
| sheath | sheathe |
| wreath | wreathe |

### 2 — Testing —
When you hear the teacher say a word from the above list, tell whether it is a verb or not. Do not look at the list.
Examples:

| T | loose | S | No |
|---|---|---|---|
|   | lose |   | Yes |
|   | prove |   | Yes |
|   | etc. |   |   |

13

3  —  Testing  —

When you hear the teacher say a word from the above list, respond with the contrasting form. Do not look at the list.

Examples:

| T | breath | S | breathe |
|---|--------|---|---------|
|   | believe |   | belief |
|   | safe |   | save |
|   | etc. |   |  |

4  —  Testing  —

Listen to the following sentences. Tell whether the word from the above list is a verb or not. Do not look at the list. Write your answers on a separate piece of paper.

Examples:

| T | She was out of *breath.* | S | No. |
|---|--------------------------|---|-----|
|   | You'll *lose* it. |   | Yes. |
|   | It's a good *excuse.* |   | No. |
|   | Try to hold your *breath.* |   |  |
|   | Do you *believe* me? |   |  |
|   | Do you have any *proof?* |   |  |
|   | *Excuse* me please. |   |  |
|   | I can *prove* it. |   |  |
|   | Do you have all your *teeth?* |   |  |
|   | We *saved* a lot of money. |   |  |
|   | Did he *close* the door? |   |  |

## II  Stress

1  —  Words in Phrases: Repetition  —

safe and sound
a savings account
a breathing exercise

prove it
seeing is believing
half and half

What a relief!
You'd better believe it.
Take a deep breath.
Save the best excuse for last.
You'll lose your life savings.

2  —  Identification  —

Read the following sentences and mark the stress. The teacher will *not* read them aloud until after you have finished.

Example:

Save me a place on the bus.

1. He never believed a word we said.
2. She's losing her teeth.

3. He brushes his teeth five times a day.
4. I'm relieved that the test is over.
5. It's safest to keep your money in a savings account.


## III  Intonation

1  — Question and Answer Review: Repetition —

Question

1. Did the pills relieve the/pain?

2. How loose is your to\oth?
3. Are you losing your/teeth?

Answer

Yes, what a relief to be rid of
  that tooth\ache.
I'm afraid it's falling o\ut.
No, I still have thirty-five\of
  them.


2  — Dialog —

Listen to the following dialog. Circle the questions with rising intonation. Underline the questions with falling intonation.


### The Dentist

Pat: What's the matter? You look awful!
Richard: It's my tooth. Or rather my teeth. That is, the teeth I had this morning.
Pat: Good Grief! I never know when you're telling the truth. Am I supposed to believe you now?
5   Richard: Seeing is believing. I'll prove it. Have a look. See? I've lost my lower two wisdom teeth.
Pat: That's only half of them. What about the other two?
Richard: Don't remind me. They've got to come out next month.


3  — Homework —

Read the following dialog and write in the appropriate stress marks and intonation lines.


### The Tooth

Richard: I've lost my tooth.
Arnold: I beg your pardon?
Richard: My tooth. I left it here on the desk. I thought it would be safe there.
Arnold: Do you think someone would steal your tooth?
5   Richard: Well, why not? Teeth are worth a lot of money these days.
Arnold: I had no idea.
Richard: Sure. You put one under your pillow and at night the good fairy comes and pays you a couple of bucks for it.
Arnold: I don't believe my ears. Are you losing your mind?
10   Richard: No, listen, it's the truth. I did this when I was a kid and it worked every time. Are you sure you haven't seen that tooth?

# LESSON SEVEN — Word Stress —

## I  Recognition and Production

### 1 — Initial Stress: Repetition —

| | | |
|---|---|---|
| téacher | míster | crówded |
| prétty | Énglish | fránkly |
| líttle | únder | cléver |
| wómen | máybe | stóry |

*Generalization: Most* English words are stressed on the first syllable.

### 2 — Stress on Second Syllable: Repetition —

*Note:* Not all words are stressed in this way. Many two syllable words, for example, are stressed on the second syllable.

| | | |
|---|---|---|
| abóut | colléct | belów |
| amóng | betwéen | garáge |
| afráid | enóugh | repéat |

### 3 — Compound Nouns: Repetition —

| | | |
|---|---|---|
| clássroom | gírlfriend | bláckboard |
| bóok store | phóne call | drúg store |
| fláshlight | póst office | týpewriter |
| téxtbook | White Hóuse | ténnis shoes |

*Generalization:* Stress on compound nouns usually falls on the first part. A compound noun is one expression made up of two nouns. But the meaning of the whole is different from merely adding the two parts. For example, *girl* and *friend* make up *girlfriend.* The compound noun may sometimes be written as two words, as in *post office.*

### 4 — Compound Noun Contrasted with Adjective + Noun: Repetition —

*Note:* The stress of compound nouns is different from the ordinary adjective and noun. Both adjective and noun are usually stressed.

16

Compound Noun                          Adjective + Noun

classroom                              big room
flashlight                             red light
girlfriend                             old friend
White House                            white house
tennis shoes                           new shoes

5 — Two Syllable Verbs: Repetition —

*Generalization:* Stress on many two syllable verbs falls on the last syllable.

believe          forget           admit
accuse           become           begin
explain          receive          advance
regard           decide           conclude
suppose          discuss          relax
repeat           assume           reduce

6 — Nouns and Verbs: Repetition —

*Generalization:* Some nouns and verbs are distinguished only by stress. The nouns receive stress on the first part; the verbs on the last part.

| Noun | Verb | Noun | Verb |
|------|------|------|------|
| increase | increase | contrast | contrast |
| permit | permit | import | import |
| progress | progress | insult | insult |
| rebel | rebel | conflict | conflict |
| suspect | suspect | incline | incline |

7 — Testing —

When you hear the teacher say a word, identify whether it is a noun or verb.
    Examples:

    T increase              S verb
       rebel                   noun
       etc.

8 — Testing —

When you hear the teacher say a word, respond with the contrasting form of that word.
    Examples:

    T permit                S permit
       contrast                contrast
       etc.

## II   Stress

### 1   — Words in Phrases: Repetition —

há́rd to explaín                      reláx and enjóy it
belié́ve it or nót                    under arrést
retúrn the boóks                     a prótest march
            You've gót to reláx.
            She belié́ves in prógress.
            The wó́rk is progréssing nícely.
            The machínes are impórted.
            They pá́y a spécial impórt-ex́port tax.

### 2   — Identification —

Read the following sentences and mark the stress. The teacher will *not* read them first.
   Example:

         She's inclí́ned to believé us.

1. I can explain everything.
2. The lawyer refused to defend him.
3. They accused him of stealing the books.
4. We decided to avoid the conflict.
5. The police arrested two suspects.

## III   Intonation

### 1   — Dialog —

Listen to the following dialog. Circle the sentences with rising intonation.

#### Letter from the Library

Richard:  How could they accuse me of stealing library books? I don't understand it.
Harriet:  In the letter they don't accuse you of stealing. It just says that you have borrowed
      over forty books and haven't returned any of them.
Richard:  Ridiculous. I'm not a forgetful person. And you know how honest I am.
5      Don't you?
Harriet:  That's why I'm inclined to be worried. Where are those books? What are you going
      to say to the people at the library?
Richard:  What do you mean "say"? The best thing to do is ignore the letter and forget all
      about it.
10   Harriet:  You'd better not. They want you to appear on Monday to explain what's
      happened.
Richard:  I may as well find a lawyer to defend me. I'm practically under arrest.
Harriet:  Relax. I'm sure you can explain everything.
Richard:  Sure. Explain it to the judge and relax in prison.

2  —  Emotions and Intonation  —

When people are upset or angry, normal stress and intonation patterns are exaggerated. The speed of speech may also vary. Listen to the dialog again. Underline the sentences which seem to have exaggerated stress and intonation. Who speaks most of these?

The verbal cues for emotional distress vary from language to language. You can learn to detect them in English if you listen carefully. Make a tape recording of two native speakers performing this dialog. Turn the sound down so you can't hear the words and listen just to the intonation patterns.

3  —  Homework  —

Read the following dialog and write in the stress and intonation lines. Be prepared to perform the dialog in class. Compare Richard's speech patterns with the previous dialog.

With the Librarian

Librarian:  Good Afternoon. May I help you with something?

Richard:  Good Afternoon. Are you Mrs. Brooks? I received a notice to see you about some books. I'm Richard Crosby . . .

Librarian:  Oh, yes. I recall the name. Won't you sit down?

5  Richard:  Thank you. I just wanted to say that, uh, the missing books . . . Well, it's a long story. But I assure you I'm innocent. I can explain everything.

Librarian:  Relax, Mr. Crosby. You're not under arrest, you know. But I admit I'd like to know why you haven't returned our books.

Richard:  I nearly returned them, but I forgot, you see. When my wife put the suitcase back
10     in the closet, that is.

Librarian:  Pardon me? Would you explain that again please.

Richard:  Certainly. I was going to return the books last month. I put them all in a suitcase. But at the last minute I forgot to take the suitcase to school. Then Harriet put the suitcase back in the closet. After that I forgot all about the books until I received your
15     notice.

Librarian:  Well, I've never heard that excuse before. So now you're returning all the books?

Richard:  Yes. Do I have to pay a fine?

Librarian:  I'm afraid so. But maybe we can reduce it a little. A story like yours deserves some reward.

**LESSON EIGHT** — Unstressed Vowels —


**I    Recognition and Production**

*Generalization:* In many words of more than one syllable the unstressed vowel is reduced to the /ə/ sound. This is the sound in such words as open, student, and section.


1  — The /ə/ Sound: Repetition —
The vowels in bold type in the following words are reduced in normal speech.

| | | |
|---|---|---|
| business | between | develop |
| beneath | correct | status |
| person | occasional | achievement |


2  — Identification —
Listen to the following sentences. Underline the reduced vowel letters.
Example:
The students are absent.


1. He broke the machine.
2. It's your problem.
3. He wasn't successful.
4. She got no presents for Christmas.
5. Serious students occasionally develop neuroses.


3  — Verb Endings: Repetition —


*Note:* The endings -ed, -en, and -ing are not normally stressed.

| | | |
|---|---|---|
| speaking | broken | reported |
| assisted | avoiding | spoken |


4  — The /ə/ Sound in Stressed Syllables: Repetition —


*Note:* The /ə/ sound may also be heard in stressed syllables.

The vowels in bold type are unstressed.

| | |
|---|---|
| enóugh | prodúction |
| fúnction | súmmon |
| condúct | Lóndon |

5  —  Nouns and Verbs: Repetition  —

---

*Generalization:*  Some of the words that change from noun to verb by a change of stress also undergo a change in vowel. When stress leaves a syllable the vowel is reduced to /ə/.

---

The vowels in bold type are unstressed.

| Noun | Verb |
|---|---|
| rébel | rebél |
| cónflict | conflíct |
| cónduct | condúct |
| cónvert | convért |
| prógress | progréss |
| prótest | protést |
| récord | recórd |

6  —  Testing  —

Listen to the following words. *Underline* the unstressed syllables. Answers are given at the end of this lesson.

Examples:

| | | | | |
|---|---|---|---|---|
| T | rébel (noun) | | S | reb**el** |
| | recórd (verb) | | | r**e**cord |

1. rebel      _____
2. protest     _____
3. convert     _____
4. conflict     _____
5. record      _____
6. conduct    _____

7  —  Testing  —

The teacher will read words from the list of noun-verbs above. When you hear a word, respond with the contrasting form.

Examples:

| | | | |
|---|---|---|---|
| T | rébel | S | rebél |
| | recórd | | récord |
| | progréss | | |
| | cónvert | | |
| | etc. | | |

8  —  Identification  —

Read the following sentences. Find the words from the noun-verb list, mark them for stress and underline their unstressed syllables. Be prepared to say whether a word is a noun or a verb.

Examples:

They made no prógre̲ss. ("Progress" is a noun.)
She re̲córded her own voice. ("Recorded" is a verb.)

1. We listened to records.
2. They joined in the protest march.
3. They rebelled against the government.
4. His conduct is terrible.
5. She was converted to another religion.
6. He had a conflict with his advisor.

## II  Stress

1  —  Words in Phrases: Repetition  —

appárently nót
demánd an apólogy
corréct your mistákes
a distínguished philósopher
pérsonal ínsult

betwéen the ácts
a prótest march
condúct a súrvey
a reásonable prótest
a recórded annóuncement

2  —  Identification  —

Read the following sentences and mark the stressed syllables. The teacher will *not* read them first.

Example:

Please corréct your mistákes.

1. They have similar records.
2. They demanded an apology.
3. It only takes a minute to record this song.
4. No additional progress has been reported.
5. I've had enough of philosophy.
6. We protested against the increase in income taxes.

## III    Intonation

1  —  Dialog  —
Listen to the following dialog. Be prepared to identify intonation patterns.


### Mr. Crosby's Application

Prof. deFrump:  His record, though not terribly distinguished, indicates to me that he can do
graduate work satisfactorily. In the last year and a half his progress has been remarkable.
Prof. Warburn:  Some members of the committee appear to be a little concerned with a
number of apparent weaknesses in his background. You don't seem to be worried about
5       that.
Prof. deFrump:  Not at all. Perhaps, as an undergraduate, he showed a certain tendency to
avoid the basic required courses. But now I'm convinced that he's a serious student with
a good chance of succeeding in this department.


2  —  Homework  —
Read the following dialog and write in the stress marks and intonation lines.


### The Faculty Decision

Prof. Lurchmint:  We seem to be agreed about all the applicants except for this fellow
Richard Crosby. DeFrump, I believe you support him.
Prof. deFrump:  I think he's capable of doing superior work.
Prof. Lurchmint:  No one else seems to think he is a serious candidate. He may just not
5       be adequately prepared for graduate work.
Prof. deFrump:  I think we should take a chance.
Prof. Lurchmint:  It's my opinion that we should admit him on special status only. Let's
inform him that he can enroll as a special student. He'll be permitted to have one
semester in which to prove that he's capable of doing the job.


Answers to I 6

| | |
|---|---|
| 1. rebel (verb) | 4. conflict (verb) |
| 2. protest (verb) | 5. record (noun) |
| 3. convert (noun) | 6. conduct (noun) |

# LESSON NINE — Unstressed Vowels and Register —

## I   Recognition and Production

### 1 — More Unstressed Vowels: Repetition —
The vowels in bold type are unstressed.

| | | |
|---|---|---|
| decísion | fináncial | suppóse |
| agréed | hónestly | concérned |
| admítted | quéstion | provísionally |
| spécial | áverage | awárded |
| assístance | appóintment | permítted |

### 2 — Light Stress: Repetition —

*Note:* Not all vowel sounds that fail to receive heavy stress ( ′ ) are reduced to the /ə/ sound. Some vowels receive lighter stress and still keep their distinctive sound.

The symbol ( ` ) indicates light stress.

| | |
|---|---|
| àcadémic | sàtisfáctory |
| àbsolútely | howèver |
| índicàte | féllòwship |
| ùnivérsity | sátisfìed |

### 3 — Compound Nouns: Repetition —

*Note:* Compound Nouns (see Lesson 7) are usually heavily stressed on the first part. But some compound nouns are marked with light stress as well as heavy stress.

| Heavy Stress | Light and Heavy Stress |
|---|---|
| bóok store | sùmmer jób |
| Chrístmas tree | Chrìstmas bónus |
| hót dog | àpple píe |
| potáto chips | chìcken soúp |
| tuítion fee | stùdent aíd |
| píng pong | gòvernment corrúption |
| chéese cake | wìnter spórts |

24

**II    Stress**

> *Generalization:* Modals and other auxiliary verbs are usually stressed when they appear with *not.*

1  —  Repetition  —

I don't like it.                              We won't have time.
We haven't finished.                          You shouldn't eat so quickly.
They aren't going to leave.                    You mustn't give up too soon.
          Pat can't go at all.
          He says he hasn't had time.
          Harriet won't accept any new students.

2  —  Identification  —
Listen to the following sentences. Identify whether the sentence is affirmative or negative.
  Examples:

      T    Dick couldn't get a fellowship.          S    Negative
           Lurch is a very nice fellow.                   Affirmative

1. The university has/hasn't considered the application.
2. Dick could/couldn't get a fellowship for next year.
3. Tuition is/isn't very expensive.
4. Some of us are/aren't eager to go to school.
5. They said we should/shouldn't worry about it.
6. Some of us can/can't go to school without a fellowship.

**III    Register**

> *Generalization:*  The English you hear and use may differ somewhat according to the social
> situation. In all formal situations, such as: when you write, when you speak with older
> people, government officials, well-educated persons, etc. you will probably use formal
> English. You may use more long, Latin-based words with many unstressed syllables.

1  —  Formal Register  —
Listen to the following dialog.

Admission to Graduate School

Richard:  Dr. Lurchmint, I believe I have an appointment to see you about my application
   **to the graduate program.**
Lurchmint:  Oh, yes. You must be Richard Crosby. Please sit down. The committee has

acted on your request to be admitted, but I am not sure you will be pleased with the
5      decision. We would like to have you enter, but you would be placed on special status.
   Richard:  Special status? Does that mean I've been awarded some kind of financial
      assistance? I certainly could use the money.
   Lurchmint:  Oh, no, I'm afraid not. As a matter of fact, financial assistance is absolutely
      out of the question at the present time. You see, "special status" indicates that the
10     department is concerned about certain weaknesses in your academic background,
      and . . .
   Richard:  But my grade point average has always been satisfactory.
   Lurchmint:  Well, uh, yes, uh, satisfactory. Nevertheless, we would like to have you enroll
      provisionally—for one semester. After that semester, if the faculty decides you have
15     made good progress, you will be allowed to continue as a regular student.
   Richard:  I know I can do a good job. But if there is no hope for a fellowship, do you
      suppose I might hope for a reduction in tuition?
   Lurchmint:  I regret to say that that is impossible for a special student. However, if you
      become a regular student, you will be eligible for all types of student aid.


2  —  Casual Register  —

---

*Generalization:*  When you speak with friends, your English will probably be more casual.
   There will be fewer long words and fewer complicated structures.

---

Listen to the following dialog.

### Harriet Gets the News

   Richard:  Honey, guess what?
   Harriet:  You found a job! Is that it?
   Richard:  No, even better than that. I was admitted to graduate school at C.U.
   Harriet:  Oh, well. I guess that that's good news. But I thought you told me you didn't have
5      a chance of getting in.
   Richard:  I didn't. Frumpie must have put in a good word for me at the committee
      meeting.
   **Harriet:  Did you talk to him today?**
   Richard:  No, I talked to old Lurch himself. I'm a "special student"—but not special enough
10     to get any money out of the school. "Absolutely out of the question at the present time,"
      he said, the old windbag.
   Harriet:  Oh, no! This means that we'll be broke for years to come. Are you sure this is a
      good idea?
   Richard:  Listen, it won't be so bad. I'm positive I'll get a fellowship after the first term. And
15     after graduation I'll be making tons of money.
   Harriet:  I'll believe it when I see it.

3  —  Homework Questions  —

Answer the following questions. Make your answers short. One or two sentences are enough.
Be prepared to discuss in class.

1.  Does the language in Dialog 1 differ from the language in Dialog 2?
    How does it differ?
2.  What is a special student?
3.  Is Harriet pleased with the news or not? How does she express her feelings?
4.  Is Richard a good student? Why do you think so?

# LESSON TEN — Grammatical Endings —

## I Grammatical Endings

*Generalization:* The so-called "s-ending" occurs at the end of 1) regular verbs, third person singular, 2) regular noun plurals, and 3) possessives. The ending has three different forms.

/s/    after voiceless consonant sounds
/z/    after voiced consonants and vowels
/əz/  after /č/ /š/ /ž/ /z/ /s/ /ǰ/

### 1 — Verbs, Third Person Singular: Repetition —

| /s/ | /z/ | /əz/ |
|-----|-----|------|
| consists | decides | raises |
| accepts | believes | chooses |
| forgets | includes | arranges |
| attacks | begins | finishes |
| reports | measures | discusses |
| presents | goes | catches |
| hopes | carries | advises |
| looks | relies | announces |

### 2 — Testing —

When you hear the teacher say the infinitive form of the verb, respond with the third person singular.

| T | | S | |
|---|---|---|---|
| | to consist | | consists |
| | to accept | | accepts |
| | to choose | | chooses |
| | to attack | | |
| | to begin | | |
| | to measure | | |
| | etc. | | |

### 3 — Identification —

Listen to the teacher read the following sentences. Identify whether the verb ends with the /s/, /z/, or /əz/ sound and write in your answer. Be prepared to say in class why the verb takes the ending it does.
Examples:

T    She *hopes* to go.              S    _s_ (because it comes after a voiceless consonant)

He *believes* us.                        _z_ (because it comes after a voiced consonant)

He *catches* a cold every winter.  _z_ (because it comes after the /č/ sound)

1. It *looks* like rain.                        ____
2. She *finishes* her work early.               ____
3. He *advises* students.                        ____
4. It *includes* everything.                     ____
5. He *reports* the news each morning.           ____
6. It *rains* every day.                          ____


4 — Practice: Read and Look Up —
Read the following sentences to yourself, then *look up* and say them. Be prepared to say
which endings the verbs take.

1. He forgets everything.
2. It just goes to show you.
3. It catches fire easily.
4. She relies on the textbook.
5. It raises the standard of living.
6. She always announces her arrival.


5 — Regular Noun Plurals: Repetition —

| /s/ | /z/ | /əz/ |
|-----|-----|------|
| events | opinions | busses |
| steaks | hotels | lunches |
| defeats | radios | sandwiches |
| strikes | managers | bridges |
| pipes | blackboards | exercises |
| boots | bees | licenses |
| tickets | thousands | garages |


6 — Testing —
When you hear the singular form of the noun, respond with the plural.
   Examples:

| T | event | S | events |
|---|-------|---|--------|
|   | hotel |   | hotels |
|   | match |   | matches |
|   | ticket |   |  |
|   | radio |   |  |
|   | lunch |   |  |
|   | etc. |   |  |


7 — Identification —
Listen to the following sentences. Identify whether the nouns end with the /s/, /z/, or /əz/ sounds.
Write in your answers. Be prepared to say why the nouns take the endings they do.
   Examples:

   T   The *busses* aren't running.   S   __əz__ (because it comes after the /s/ sound)
       The *pipes* are frozen.            __s__ (because it comes after a voiceless consonant)

this exercise continued on next page

1. The city has a lot of *bridges.* ____
2. Political *events* are often surprising. ____
3. *Televisions* are cheap here. ____
4. My *hands* are cold. ____
5. *Peaches* are delicious. ____
6. The *pots* and *pans* are in the cupboard. ____

8 — Practice: Read and Look Up —

Read the following sentences to yourself, then *look up* and say them. Be prepared to say what endings the nouns take.

1. She eats two steaks each morning for breakfast.
2. Our opinions carry some weight.
3. These radios aren't for sale.
4. We ran out of matches.
5. The knives are in the drawer.
6. Where do we buy the tickets?

9 — Possessives: Repetition —

| /s/ | /z/ | /əz/ |
|---|---|---|
| Pete's new car | Ann's new apartment | Alice's new television |
| Phillip's car | Bill's new apartment | George's new television |
| Eric's car | Jerry's new apartment | Harris' new television |
| the cop's car | the woman's apartment | the judge's new television |

10 — Practice —

Repeat: Alice's new car is right outside.

Substitue: 
| T | | S | |
|---|---|---|---|
| | Phillip / new car | | Phillip's new car is right outside. |
| | Mohammed / motocycle | | Mohammed's motorcycle is right outside. |
| | Jose / mother-in-law | | Jose's mother-in-law is right outside. |
| | (Alice) / bicycle | | |
| | (Jose) / new car | | |
| | (Pradit) / brother | | |
| | (Miguel) / lawyer | | |
| | (Rich) / motorcycle | | |
| | (Nikola) / girlfriend | | |

11   —   Practice: Read and Look Up   —
Read the following sentences to yourself, then *look up* and say them aloud.

1. Pete's new car is really nice.
2. What's Ann's new address?
3. You can't rely on Alice's husband.
4. It wasn't the cop's fault.
5. Jerry's mother isn't home.
6. It was the judge's decision.

## II   Stress

1   —   Words in Phrases: Repetition   —

plane tickets                 knives and forks            dirty looks
tests and quizzes            favorite things             clocks and watches
used cars                    likes and dislikes          hopes and fears

Buy your tickets at the door.
Arnold shines his shoes with old toothbrushes.
He reads thousands of pages a week.

2   —   Identification   —
Listen to the following sentences and mark the stressed words.
    Example:

She sells tickets at the door.

1. He listens to the news every day.
2. Drivers' licenses expire on people's birthdays.
3. She always forgets her shoes and socks.
4. He relaxes at least twelve hours a day.
5. She fires half her employees every six months.

## III   Intonation

1   —   Repetition   —

| Question | Answer |
|---|---|
| 1. Whose car is that? | It's George's. |
| 2. Does the price include utilities? | Yes, it includes everything. |
| 3. How often does she go to concerts? | She attends every performance. |
| 4. Does he play with his chopsticks? | No, he uses them to eat with. |

### 2 — Question and Answer Chain (Plurals) —

| | | | |
|---|---|---|---|
| S1 | What does (Armando) like to eat? | S2 | He likes *carrots.* |
| S2 | What does he like to eat? | S3 | He likes *carrots and hot dogs.* |
| S3 | What does he like to eat? | S4 | He likes *carrots and hot dogs and eggs.* |

etc.

### 3 — Question and Answer Chain (Possessives) —

| | | | |
|---|---|---|---|
| S1 | Whose things did (Amir) steal? | S2 | He stole *Alice's glasses.* |
| S2 | Whose things did he steal? | S3 | He stole *Alice's glasses and Mohammed's cigarettes.* |

etc.

### 4 — Homework —

Read the following sentences and write in the stress marks and intonation lines. The italicized words have s-endings. For each one write down whether it has the /s/, /z/, or /əz/ sound. Be prepared to say in class why each one takes the sound it does.

Example:

He *likes* to drink good strong whisky.                                   s

1. Buy your *tickets* early.                                                    ___
2. It *looks* like rain.                                                        ___
3. He (a) *uses* (b) *matches* to light his (c) *cigarettes.*        a) ___  b) ___  c) ___
4. Alice (a) *cooks* (b) *steaks* as tough as (c) *boots.*          a) ___  b) ___  c) ___
5. She (a) *carries* (b) *boxes* of (c) *groceries* upstairs.       a) ___  b) ___  c) ___

# LESSON ELEVEN — Intonation in Compound Sentences —

## I Voiced / Voiceless Contrasts (Singular to Plural)

> *Generalization:* In some nouns the change from singular to plural is accompanied by a change in the final sounds from voiceless to voiced.

### 1 — Repetition —

| Singular (voiceless) | Plural (voiced) | Singular (voiceless) | Plural (voiced) |
|---|---|---|---|
| loaf | loaves | thief | thieves |
| leaf | leaves | calf | calves |
| wife | wives | sheaf | sheaves |
| knife | knives | half | halves |
| sheath | sheathes | life | lives |

### 2 — Identification —
When you hear the teacher say a word, identify whether it is singular or plural.
Examples:

| T | loaf | S | singular |
|---|---|---|---|
| | wives | | plural |
| | life | | singular |
| | etc. | | |

### 3 — Testing —
When you hear the teacher say a word from the list above, respond with the contrasting word.
Examples:

| T | knife | S | knives |
|---|---|---|---|
| | half | | halves |
| | thieves | | thief |
| | etc. | | |

## II Stress

### 1 — Words in Phrases: Repetition —

loaves of bread
autumn leaves
a sharp knife

a long half-life
husbands and wives
half and half

A cat is supposed to have nine lives.
You're shaking like a leaf.
It takes a thief to catch a thief.

2  —  Identification  —

Read the following sentences and write in the stress marks. The teacher will not say these
sentences until you finish. Be prepared to read them aloud.
    Example:
        They trý to sáve móney.


1.  They don't believe their wives.
2.  Calves are just little cows.
3.  You'll have to find some proof.
4.  They spent over half their lives fighting with their wives.
5.  The prisoner received a loaf of bread with a knife inside.


III    **Intonation in Compound Sentences**


> *Generalization:* When main clauses are joined together with *and, but,* or *or,* both clauses
>     usually take falling intonation. But the intonation of the first clause does not fall as
>     low as that of the final clause.
>
> Examples:     I had an appoint\ment, but I couldn't g\o.
>               You can go to sch\ool, and I can wo\rk.


1  —  Repetition  —


1.  Each class takes two ho\urs, and there are two classes a we\ek.

2.  You can come al\ong, but don't make any no\ise.

3.  Arnold won't be ha\ppy, but that's just too ba\d.

4.  Take the book with\ you, and drop it off at the li\brary.

5.  Harriet doesn't teach sch\ool, but she has stu\dents.


2  —  Identification  —

Listen to the following main clauses. Identify by the intonation pattern whether each one is a
non-final or a final clause. (The answers are at the end of this lesson.)
    Examples:

        T    I have an appoint\ment          S    *non-final*

             I couldn't find ti\me                *final*

             We've been very bu\sy                *non-final*

             We'll try to help \you               *final*


1.  We're going downtown                    _____


2.  He forgot to buy it                      _____


**this exercise continued on next page**

3.  Richard is going to cut down expenses          _____

4.  Banana splits will have to go                  _____

5.  Richard isn't very eager to learn              _____


3  —  Identification  —
Write in the intonation lines on the following compound sentences. Your teacher will not say them
until after you have finished. Be prepared to say the sentence yourself.
   Example:
      The salary is go\od, but it's hard wo\rk.


1.  It hurts me to say it, but I'll have to get a job.

2.  I've applied for jobs, but I haven't had any interviews.

3.  You have to find a job, or we won't survive.

4.  I'm twenty-five years old, and my uncle is too.

5.  My watch stopped, and we were both late for the party.


4  —  Yes / No Questions: Repetition  —

---

*Generalization:* When two Yes / No questions are connected by the conjunction *or,* the
    intonation of the clauses is different. The first clause carries rising intonation, and
    the second one carries falling intonation.

---

1.  Are you go/ing or aren't\you?
2.  Is she a te/acher or is she a stu\dent?
3.  Are they going down/town or are they going on a pic\nic?
4.  Have they agreed to s/tay or no\t?
5.  Will he finish the pa/per or ask for an incompl\ete?


5  —  Identification  —
Write in the intonation lines on the following compound sentences. You will not hear the
sentences until you finish. Be prepared to say them aloud.
   Example:
      Are you ti/red or do you want to go to the par\ty?


1.  Did he get a job or is he still looking?
2.  Will he have to work or did he get a fellowship?
3.  Did he get a fellowship or will he have to work?
4.  Have you finished the application or are you still writing?
5.  Shall we do without food or will you find a job?

6  —  Dialog  —

Listen to the following dialog and write in the intonation lines. Be prepared to say why a sentence takes rising or falling intonation.


### Money

Richard:  Harriet, let's cut out all unnecessary expenses, and then I'll be able to study full-time.

Harriet:  Sure, sure. To begin with we could cut out grocueries and clothes. Would you like to die of starvation or would you rather freeze to death next winter?

5    Richard:  Be reasonable, Harriet. You can take a few more students, and I'll stop eating lunches.

Harriet:  I am being reasonable! Why are you being so thick-headed? Do you think lunches will make any difference? Why don't you cut out cigarettes and cigars and bourbon and records and tapes, and I'll cut out jewels and fur coats.

10   Richard:  Very funny.

Harriet:  And at the same time you could cut out doughnuts and cookies and apple pies and cheese cakes and ice cream sundaes and banana splits and . . .

Richard:  Banana splits too?

Harriet:  Why not? You might even lose a few pounds.

15   Richard:  Listen, Harriet. Why don't we use just a little of our savings. I'm sure I can make it up after I graduate.

Harriet:  Savings? What savings? Do you think we have any savings left? We've got $4.00 in the bank, and our debts total nearly $2000.00. Either you get a job, or we won't survive the winter. At least, you won't.


7  —  Homework  —

Read the following dialog and answer briefly the questions at the end. Be prepared to discuss in class.


### The Job Situation

Richard:  It hurts me to say it, but I've got to find a job. My wife is tired of working so hard, and the department refuses to give me any money for next year.

Arnold:  Maybe you could do old Lurch's laundry for him.

Miguel:  Jobs are hard to find these days. Have you filled out any applications?

5    Richard:  I've applied to dozens of places, and this week I had two interviews, but nothing came of them. I need a part-time job that pays a lot of money.

Miguel:  Don't we all!

Richard:  One of my wife's students may be able to help me find something.

Arnold:  Your wife's students? Is Harriet a school teacher?

10   Richard:  No, not really. She accepts private students, you see. She instructs a Yoga class . . .

Miguel:  Yoga!

Arnold:  You mean she teaches people to stand on their heads and that sort of thing?

Richard:  I really don't know much about it. She wants me to learn it, but I hate exercise. She wants me to do lots of things that I hate. Yoga is only one of them.

Answer briefly the following questions, using the two dialogs in III 6 and III 7.

1. What does Harriet want Richard to do?
2. What kind of mood is Harriet in? How do you know how she feels?
3. What does Richard decide to do? Is he happy about it?

Answers: III 2

1. final
2. final
3. non-final

4. non-final
5. final

# LESSON TWELVE — *-ed* Endings —

**I** *-ed* **Endings**

---

*Generalization:* The verb ending *-ed* may be pronounced in three ways:

/t/ after voiceless consonants (except **t**)

/d/ after vowels and voiced consonants (except **d**)

/əd/ after **t** or **d**

---

1 — Repetition —

| /t/ | /d/ | /əd/ |
|---|---|---|
| looked | believed | decided |
| stopped | relied | waited |
| locked | concerned | started |
| laughed | rained | accepted |
| priced | carried | avoided |
| raced | caused | defeated |
| ceased | bombed | reported |

---

*Note:* The /əd/ ending is always *unstressed*.

decíded

waíted

---

2 — Identification —

Listen to the following sentences, circle the *-ed* endings and mark whether this ending has the sound /t/, /d/, or /əd/. Be prepared to say why an ending takes the sound it does.

Examples:

| | |
|---|---|
| It rained all day. | *d* (follows voiced consonant) |
| She looked at him. | *t* (follows voiceless consonant) |
| I carried my books. | *d* (follows vowel) |
| We accepted the job. | *əd* (follows **t**) |

1. He stopped eating lunches. _____
2. We aren't concerned about money. _____
3. They avoided their old friends. _____
4. I laughed at her joke. _____
5. She waited all morning. _____
6. It caused us some concern. _____

38

3  —  Identification  —

Read the following sentences to yourself, circle the *-ed* endings and mark whether the ending
has the sound /t/, /d/, or /ə d/. Be prepared to read and look up in class.

Examples:

| They've never been defeat(ed) | ə d |
| She lock(ed) the door. | t |
| They stay(ed) all week. | d |

1. He decided to go to school next fall. ____
2. She never stopped trying. ____
3. They were admitted to graduate school. ____
4. We refused to take the job. ____
5. She accepted the fellowship. ____
6. He hasn't adjusted to the new situation. ____

## II  Stress

1  —  Words in Phrases: Repetition  —

decidéd in advánce
accépted by Colúmbia
ráted X
repórted in the *Times*

hánded in on tíme
lánded sáfely
defeáted by Pénn Státe
inclúded in the príce

He sólved the móney problem.
She avóided fínding a jób.
You're invíted to a párty at my apártment.
They lóoked awfully tíred.

2  —  Identification  —

Listen to the following sentences and write in the stress marks.

Example:

We beliéved in the pówer of móney.

1. I'm concerned about getting a job.
2. He never caused a lot of trouble.
3. We used up all our savings.
4. It was reported in all the newspapers.
5. She looked for a good job at the university.
6. He hasn't stopped trying, but he's very disappointed.

## III   Intonation

1 — Intonation Review: Repetition —

| Question | Answer |
|---|---|
| 1. You mean he got a job? | Yes, but it's only part-time. |
| 2. You mean his record wasn't very good? | No, he had mostly C's. |
| 3. You mean you laughed at Arnold? | Yes, but I didn't mean to. |
| 4. You mean he refused to take the job? | Yes, he didn't want to be a truck driver. |

2 — Dialog —

Listen to the following dialog. Be prepared to identify the intonation patterns of the sentences.

### Pat and Arnold Spread the News

Arnold:  Have you heard the latest?

Robert:  No, what?

Pat:  Dick Crosby has decided to go to grad school next fall.

Robert:  That's impossible.

5   Pat:  But it's true. The university has admitted him and he has already accepted.

Robert:  But what will he use for money? He's already borrowed a hundred dollars from me this term and he still wants more.

Arnold:  I'd like to know what that cabbagehead is going to use for brains.

Pat:  He says he's solved the money problem. At first he demanded a fellowship, and he nearly

10   refused to enter without one. Of course he was turned down.

Arnold:  Of course! He's the weakest student in the department. He probably hasn't received more than half a dozen A's since kindergarten. How could he get a fellowship?

Pat:  Even Dick finally realized it was impossible. But he will have money. His wife works, and now he's been hired to drive a school bus for some private school.

15   Robert:  Good old Dick. He never stops trying. He doesn't seem too smart, but he's always managed to get what he wants. I wonder how he does it?

Arnold:  He's always avoided using his brains—that's his secret. Sheer stupid luck.

Pat:  Arnold! I think you're jealous!

3 — Homework —

Read the following dialog and answer the questions. Be prepared to discuss in class.

### Richard and Arnold

Richard:  I know how you must feel, Arnie. Disappointed.

Arnold:  I don't think I've ever revealed to you how I feel about anything.

Richard:  Well, it's only natural. You flunked a couple of tests, handed in a crummy paper, and you failed to get an assistantship. It could've happened to anybody. I didn't get one

5   myself.

Arnold:  You weren't expected to get one.

Richard:  But I always hoped I would. I did good work for Frumpie.

Arnold:  So did I.

Richard:  Yes, but he never liked you very much . . . Look, Arnie, why don't you get a job
10    like me and go to school part-time? One of my wife's student's husbands—I mean, this
guy, the husband of one of my wife's students—has started up a construction business,
and he needs truck drivers.

Arnold:  But I'm a chemist, not a truck driver!

Richard:  Am I a bus driver? No. But I adjusted to a new situation, and now I drive a bus
15    full of kids every morning and afternoon.

Arnold:  Congratulations. I've always avoided following your example in the past, and I
see no reason to change now. Thanks for all the unwanted advice. Good-bye!

Richard:  Why does that guy get so excited? I can see he'll have to be convinced.


Questions

In answering the questions make use of both dialogs III 2 and III 3.

1. How does Arnold feel about Richard? How does he express his feelings?
2. What are some of the ways to pay for the costs of an education mentioned in the dialogs?
3. What sort of student do you think Richard was in school?

**LESSON THIRTEEN** — Intonation in Complex Sentences

**I Review of -s and -ed Endings**

1 — Testing (-ed Endings) —

When you hear the teacher say a word, respond with the -s form of the word.
   Examples:

Verb

| T | | S | |
|---|---|---|---|
| | consist | | consists |
| | decide | | decides |
| | raise | | raises |
| | begin | | |
| | advise | | |
| | catch | | |
| | hope | | |
| | go | | |
| | raise | | |
| | rely | | |
| | announce | | |

Noun

| T | | S | |
|---|---|---|---|
| | ticket | | tickets |
| | boot | | boots |
| | bridge | | bridges |
| | manager | | |
| | sandwich | | |
| | thousand | | |
| | Jerry | | |
| | Alice | | |
| | Eric | | |
| | Harris | | |
| | Ann | | |

2 — Testing (-ed Endings) —

When you hear the teacher say a word, respond with the -ed form of that word.
   Examples:

| T | | S | |
|---|---|---|---|
| | look | | looked |
| | believe | | believed |
| | wait | | waited |
| | bomb | | |
| | rely | | |
| | decide | | |
| | race | | |
| | laugh | | |
| | accept | | |
| | rain | | |
| | cause | | |

**II   Complex Sentences and Intonation**

---

*Generalization:*  A complex sentence is one containing one or more dependent clauses. Both the
main clause and dependent clauses usually take the same intonation pattern as if they were
independent sentences.

---

1  —  Complex Sentences: Repetition  —

1. When they arrive tonight they may be pretty tired.
2. If you want to buy a car, you have to get a loan.
3. We can solve the problem ourselves if we have to.
4. He wasn't given a fellowship even though his grades were good.
5. You shouldn't waste time if you want to get there early.

2  —  Practice: Read and Look Up  —

1. If you call his office you might catch him.
2. I'll go by myself if you think it's important.
3. He may have to come late because he had a test.
4. He might have won the election if he had had more money.
5. We should go to a movie despite the fact that we're broke.

---

*Note:*  In complex Yes / No questions the final clause carries rising intonation even if it is
not in question form. Examples:
>        Do you want to stay even if it's boring?
>        Shall we go even though it costs a lot of money?
In complex *Wh*-questions the final clause does *not* rise in intonation. Examples:
>        What shall we do when we get there?
>        How can he live if he doesn't have a job?

---

3  —  Repetition  —

1. Do you want to stay even if it's boring?
2. Will you graduate if you don't take the course in statistics?
3. Will you support him if he runs for office again?
4. Do you mean she won't go unless she gets the day off?
5. Have you decided to take the job even though you don't like the boss?

4  —  Read and Look up  —

1. May we open the gift even though it's not Christmas yet?
2. If you want to get all A's you have to study all the time.

this exercise continued on next page

3. If it rains do you want to take the car?
4. Shall we talk to him when he finally gets here?
5. We should have handed in the paper even though it wasn't finished.
6. If he refuses to listen shall we tell him to leave?
7. We might have enough money for ice cream if we stop smoking cigarettes.
8. Can you graduate in a year if you take four courses a term?
9. Will you be here tomorrow even if you don't feel well?
10. Can we find an apartment in this town if we don't want to sign a lease?

5   —   Dialog and Homework   —
Listen to the following dialog and answer the questions at the end.


### Richard Stands on his Head

Richard:  I know I should practice today, hon, and I would if my back weren't so sore
from yesterday. Let's skip the lesson today.

Harriet:  Dick, you can't skip lessons if you want to make any progress. When you don't
do the exercises every day you don't get the full benefits.

5      Richard:  But I got the full benefits yesterday. I can still feel them—in my arms, my legs,
my back, my elbows, my shoulders. I'm full of benefits.

Harriet:  Don't be silly. If you keep at it every day you won't feel any soreness. Now let
me show you the headstand again. Put your hands together like this. Dick, pay
attention! You could have stood alone yesterday if you had had your hands in the

10      right position. Now when you raise your left leg, don't go too far or you may fall
over. But don't worry because I'll catch your leg if you start to fall. Now you try it.

Richard:  Listen, sweetheart, is this really necessary? Enough blood rushes to my head
even when I stand up.

Harriet:  Don't look for excuses. Once you can do it yourself you'll love the headstand.
15      It's a splendid exercise.

Richard:  Now when I put my hands together where do I put my elbows? Like this?

Harriet:  That's fine. Now lift your left leg up. OK.

Richard:  If I move my elbow will I fall over? It hurts.

Harriet:  Don't talk, silly. I can't understand you when you're upside down. Now bring
20      the other leg up. No, not like that! Don't move your elbows!


### CRASH!

Richard:  Oooooooh, my knee.

Harriet:  Dick, are you all right?

Richard:  I thought you were going to catch my leg if I started to fall.

Harriet:  Well, you didn't follow directions. And you nearly knocked over my Chinese
25      vase! If your knee hadn't hit that table, you would have destroyed that vase. Dick
we're really lucky.

Richard:  I don't feel so lucky.

Harriet:  Well, there's no sense in feeling sorry for yourself. Come on, let's try it again.
You almost did it that time.

Homework questions
Answer each question briefly. Be prepared to discuss in class.

1. What is Harriet's opinion of the exercise?
2. Even before the accident, was Dick eager to practice?
3. How do you do the exercise?
4. Does Harriet use any words that are typical of women's speech?
   Does Richard use any words typical of men's speech?

## LESSON FOURTEEN — Falling Intonation and Stress

### I  Stress and Intonation

> *Generalization:*  In some sentences which take falling intonation, the intonation falls directly on the final syllable of the sentence. This occurs when the final syllable is one which would normally be stressed. Examples:
>
> Give it to George.
> He wants to work.

1 —  Repetition  —

1. I have to leave.
2. What would you like to eat?
3. I don't think he's really the coach.
4. It depends on whether we have room.
5. That couldn't be true.

*Note:*  What are the kinds of words that are normally stressed? See Lesson Three.

2 —  Identification  —

Listen to the following sentences and write in the intonation lines. Example:

He'll probably forget to come.

1. What did you forget?
2. How much does it cost?
3. What did you tell them to do?
4. He says he likes living in New York.
5. He said he failed because he hadn't prepared.

> *Generalization:*  In some sentences that take falling intonation the intonation falls *between* syllables. This occurs when the last syllable of the sentence is not stressed; the intonation falls after the last stressed syllable. Examples:
>
> He's my brother.
> Let's call him.

3 —  Repetition  —

1. How did you do it?
2. When are we leaving?

this exercise continued on next page

3. She didn't bring any‾\thing.
4. He has a good appe‾\tite.
5. What are you going to do‾\ with it?


4  —  Identification  —
Listen to the following sentences and write in the intonation lines.
    Example:
        You'll have to give it back‾\ to him.


1. When did you talk to him?
2. Everybody says he's honest.
3. No one was inclined to believe us.
4. She left all the letters unwritten.
5. He took one look at it before he refused to eat it.


5  —  Identification  —
Read the following sentences and write in the intonation lines. The teacher will not say the
sentences until you have finished.
    Examples:
                I don't believe\ it.
                Arnold has a good vo‾\ice.


1. Harriet won't take any new students.
2. Tell her to wait for us at home.
3. We don't have anything to eat, but we're still very happy.
4. Why don't you leave your name and address, and we'll call you later.
5. I would have been here on time, but there wasn't a parking place.


## II  Particles and Prepositions

*Generalization:* Particles are sometimes stressed. When a sentence ends with a verb and a
    particle, the particle is the last stressed syllable. Intonation will thus fall on the particle.
        Examples:

                    Who should we call‾\ up?
                    I don't know how to turn it o\n.


1  —  Repetition  —


1. Which one did you pick o‾\ut?
2. Gus thought he wouldn't show u\p.
3. If you don't know what the word means, look it u‾\p.
4. I'd like to have some time to think it ov‾\er.
5. Tell me when you want me to give it ba‾\ck.

*Generalization:* If a sentence ends with a verb and preposition, the preposition is not stressed. Intonation will thus fall before the preposition.

Examples:

Who shall I write \to?

There's nothing to look \at.

---

2  —  Repetition  —

1. What are you looking \for?
2. It's not the job Arnold was dreaming \of.
3. I forgot the name of the man I have to write \to.
4. I don't know what Dick was thinking \of.
5. That's what we're writing our papers \on.

3  —  Identification  —

Listen to the following sentences and identify whether they end in a particle or a preposition.

Examples:

| T | What are you working \on? | S | Preposition |
|   | You'll have to look it u\p. |   | Particle |

1. She didn't show up.
2. Who's the guy you're working for?
3. Why did Arnold want to turn him down?
4. It doesn't matter what you think up.
5. Sure you can borrow it, but don't forget to bring it back.

4  —  Identification  —

Listen to the following sentences and write in the intonation lines. Be prepared to identify whether the sentence ends in a particle or a preposition.

Examples:

What were you thinking \of?

Speaking is something he's very good \at.

She asked me to pick it o\ut.

1. I don't feel like calling him up.
2. "Gus" is the name I was thinking of.
3. She wanted to check the book out just as I was bringing it back.
4. I don't know what you're talking about.
5. I'm not sure what he was looking at, but I know what he was thinking of.

5   —   Dialog   —

Listen to the following dialog. Be prepared to identify intonation patterns and answer the questions at the end.

Arnold's Interview

Arnold:  Excuse me. I believe you're the man I'm looking for. My name is Arnold Bixby. I came to apply for a job.

Gus:  Oh, sure. The boss told me you was coming. My name's Gus. I'm the foreman here, and I do the hiring. I thought you wasn't goin' to show up.

5   Arnold:  I tried to call you, but I couldn't get through. I wanted to cancel our appointment.

Gus:  What happened? You find a job already?

Arnold:  No, I'm still looking, but construction work is just something I'm not qualified for.

10   Gus:  This here's the office. Go on in and set yourself down. What do they call you anyway? Arnie?

Arnold:  People call me Arnold.

Gus:  OK, Arnold. Now what's this all about? The boss told me you wanted a job real bad.

Arnold:  Well, it's true I need a part-time job.

15   Gus:  You mean you can't work full-time?

Arnold:  No, I have to go to school too.

Gus:  School! Boy, they couldn't get me to go back to school if they paid me.

Arnold:  Believe me, they're not paying anybody.

Gus:  What do you study over there at the university?

20   Arnold:  I'm in chemistry.

Gus:  Afraid we ain't got no jobs for chemists here. But we could put you on as a cement-mixer. How's that?

Arnold:  You must be putting me on. Look, this is some kind of mistake. I let myself get talked into this by Dick Crosby, but. . . .

25   Gus:  Never heard of him. Tell me, Arnie, what kind of experience you had? What kind of things you good at?

Arnold:  Well, I once wrote for my high school newspaper, and I do know how to play the violin, and my mother says. . . .

Gus:  Arnie, I like you. You got a sense of humor. Sit down and we'll talk this over. I

30   think we can find you something.

Questions

1. Does Gus speak ''good'' English? Explain. Give examples.
2. How does Gus feel about first names? How does Arnold feel?
3. Is Arnold eager to get this job? Explain.

# LESSON FIFTEEN — Review —

## I  Sound Contrasts; Intonation Patterns

### 1 — Repetition —

| | | | | | |
|---|---|---|---|---|---|
| thank | sank | tank | breathe | breeze | breed |
| thin | sin | tin | writhe | rise | ride |
| | | | | | |
| path | pass | pat | then | Zen | den |
| tenth | tense | tent | though | | dough |

| | |
|---|---|
| ether | either |
| teeth | teethe |
| wreath | wreathe |

### 2 — Falling Intonation — Question and Answer —
Example:

S1   What's that?       S2   That's a thermometer.

Ask (Carlos) what this (point to object) is.
Ask (    ) what these are.
Ask (    ) what those are.
Ask (    ) how many brothers he / she has.
Ask (    ) where his father and mother first met.
Ask (    ) what he / she thinks of this university.

## II  Sound Contrasts; Rhythm

### 1 — Repetition —

| /s/ | /z/ | /b/ | /v/ |
|---|---|---|---|
| Sue | zoo | boat | vote |
| sewn | zone | best | vest |
| sink | zinc | marble | marvel |
| lacy | lazy | cupboard | covered |
| ice | eyes | curb | curve |
| ceasing | seizing | | |

2  —  Repetition  —

an éasy ánswer                          Pléase páss the toást.
búy the véry bést                       You're dríving me crázy.
búy tíckets in advánce                  Hów's the wéather in Mississíppi?

3  —  Identification  —

Read the sentences and mark the stressed words. Be prepared to say what kind of words are
stressed. (See Lesson 3)
    Example:
        He boúght it to gíve to his móther.

1.  He always buys the very best beer.
2.  The teacher says all our questions are stupid.
3.  She's got a lot of money.
4.  We refused to sign the lease.
5.  Pat forgot to vote in the last election.

## III  More Sound Contrasts; -s and -ed Endings

1  —  Repetition  —

| Noun | Verb (voiced) | | Adjective | Verb (voiced) |
|------|---------------|---|-----------|---------------|
| belief | believe | | close | close |
| proof | prove | | loose | lose |
| excuse | excuse | | safe | save |
| strife | strive | | | |

| Singular | Plural (voiced) |
|----------|-----------------|
| wife | wives |
| knife | knives |
| shelf | shelves |
| leaf | leaves |
| loaf | loaves |

2  —  The -s Endings: Repetition  —
/s/, /z/, and /əz/ (See Lesson 10)

1.  Sue's grades made her parents very happy.
2.  Good cooks are always collecting recipes.
3.  San Francisco's many bridges are very lovely.

this exercise continued on next page

4. George's mistakes cost us hundreds of dollars.
5. Every ticket he loses costs us a fortune.


3 — Read and Look Up —

Read the following sentences to yourself, then *look up* and say them aloud. Be prepared to say
whether each *-s* ending is the /s/, /z/, or /əz/ sound.
    Example:

        Alice's cats are horrid little demons.
      S     Alice's     /əz/
               cats       /s/
               demons   /z/


1. He always forgets his gloves.
2. Bob's glasses broke into thousands of pieces.
3. She leaves some scraps for the dogs.
4. Richard fills out two job applications a day.
5. He promises to talk to one of Harriet's students.


4 — The *-ed* endings: Repetition —
/t/, /d/, and /əd/ (See Lesson 12)
Write down the *ed*-words and identify the sound.
    Example:

        Arnold refused to look for jobs.           refus*ed*    /d/ _____


1. Then he allowed himself to be talked into it.    _____
2. But he lacked experience.    _____
3. He was disappointed, but he accepted the job.    _____
4. We regarded the case as closed.    _____
5. They were disappointed when we stopped giving away money.    _____


5 — The *-s* endings and the *-ed* endings: Read and Look Up —


1. She closed all the windows.
2. He couldn't be convicted without proof.
3. The leaves haven't changed their colors yet.
4. We saved our excuses for the judge.
5. He refused to believe any of his wives.
6. She says she's reserved seats for us.
7. I was excused from all my classes.
8. They were permitted to shine Lurch's shoes.

## IV  Stress; Yes / No Question Intonation

1  —  Repetition  —

| Compound Noun | Adjective + Noun |
|---|---|
| cláss̀room | a bíg roòm |
| boók store | a niće stóre |
| bláckboard | a bláck boárd |
| gírl friend | a goód friénd |

2  —  Repetition  —

| Noun | Verb |
|---|---|
| íncrease | increáse |
| pérmit | permít |
| súspect | suspéct |
| ímport | impórt |
| íncline | inclíne |

3  —  Read and Look Up  —

Practice the questions and answers in pairs; read them, then look up and say them aloud.

| Question | Answer |
|---|---|
| 1. Are the textbooks printed in New York? | No, they're all imported. |
| 2. His girlfriend did it? | No, but she is suspected by the police. |
| 3. Has the book store raised its prices? | Yes, import costs have increased. |
| 4. The truck driver was arrested? | Yes, he failed to get a permit. |
| 5. Don't you trust landlords? | Landlords are not to be trusted. |
| 6. Did you look up the answer? | No, we weren't permitted to use our books. |
| 7. Have you decided to stay on the job? | Yes, they increased our salaries. |
| 8. Are you shopping for gifts? | Yes, but there aren't any bargains. |

4  —  Guessing Game  —

Try to guess the *hobby* of one of your fellow students. Ask only Yes / No questions. The person interviewed should answer only with *yes* or *no*.

Examples:

| | | | |
|---|---|---|---|
| S1 | Do you practice your hobby indoors? | S2 | Yes |
| S3 | Does it cost much money? | S2 | No |
| | etc. | | |

**V   Reduced Vowels; Compound & Complex Sentences**

1  —  Reduced Vowels: (See Lesson 8) Repetition —
Vowels in bold type are unstressed.

|  |  |
|---|---|
| profess**io**n | kitch**e**n |
| corr**e**ct | cem**e**nt |
| devel**o**p | reduct**io**n |
| pers**o**n | supp**o**rt |
| stud**e**nt | therm**o**s |

2  —  Identification —
Listen to the following sentences and mark the unstressed, *reduced vowels* by *underlining*.
Example:

Some pers**o**ns are not stud**e**nts.

1. He's a successful person.
2. Students are often disappointed.
3. The professor hasn't finished correcting the papers.
4. They were awarded prizes for their solutions to the problem.
5. She's been developing new textbooks for the school children in Nevada.

3  —  Compound Sentences (See Lesson 11): Read and Look Up  —
Examples:

We'll attend the mee\ting, but wè'll be la\te.

Let's talk\to her, and then we'll dec\ide.

Shall we leave⌡now, or shall we stay for din\ner?

1. I'm going to do it, but I don't like it.
2. We have to leave now, or we'll miss the bus.
3. Are we going, or aren't we?
4. He says he hasn't had time to do the job, but actually he has.
5. We won't have much time, but we should stop at your mother's house.
6. I always wanted to see the movie, and now I'm going to.
7. Would you like a drink, or have you given up martinis?
8. She won't take any more new students, but we might.

4  —  Practice: Make An Excuse  —

Suppose someone asks you to do something you don't like, and you have to make an excuse.
Use compound sentences, as in the example. Examples:

| | | | |
|---|---|---|---|
| T | eat more ice cream | S | I'd like to eat more ice cream, (but I've just started a new diet). |
| | work Saturday mornings | | I would love to work Saturday mornings, (but I have to visit my mother in the hospital). |

do more homework
stop eating banana splits
do more Yoga exercise
find another part-time job
write another paper
make a speech
go to the dentist
learn another language
take a course in economics

5  —  Complex Sentences (See Lesson 13): Read and Look Up  —
Examples:

If the dog bite\s you, give it a ki\ck.
Will you wait/ here, even if I'm/ late?
Are you going to/ school, even if they don't give you a _fe/llowship?

1.  Do you want him to call you even if he comes in late?
2.  Even if I inherited a million dollars I wouldn't lend him a quarter.
3.  Would you like to borrow my copy in case the book store doesn't have one?
4.  Even though you like him personally, would you vote for him?
5.  You won't have anything to eat next winter unless you get a job.
6.  You mean you won't accept him until he improves his grades?
7.  We won't have a good time unless you come along too.
8.  Although we approve of his decision we still don't like him.

6  —  Practice: What Would You Do?  —
Examples:

| | | | |
|---|---|---|---|
| T | if it snowed today | S1 | What would you do if it snowed today? |
| | | S2 | (I would probably go skiing.) |
| | if you failed an exam | S2 | What would you do if you failed an exam? |
| | | S3 | (I would buy a ticket to fly home.) |

this exercise continued on next page

if your rent were increased
if you found somebody's wallet
if your family ordered you to go home
if your apartment building burned down
if you didn't receive a check from home
if you were offered a job in New York
if your wallet were stolen
if your teachers went on strike

# LESSON SIXTEEN — /i/ /iy/ —

## I  Recognition and Production

### 1  — Repetition —

| | | | |
|---|---|---|---|
| sit | seat | will | we'll |
| fit | feet | tin | teen |
| still | steal | his | he's |
| slip | sleep | it | eat |
| sick | seek | hit | heat |
| mill | meal | list | least |

## II  Stress

### 1  — Repetition —

| | | |
|---|---|---|
| eát a peách | get ríd of it | gíve me a hínt |
| to eách his ówn | a líttle bit | éasy líving |
| thrée méals a wéek | a shópping list | hóliday gréetings |
| an éasterly breéze | gíve it a kíck | a wínning téam |

Can you gíve me a hínt?
We eát our méals from tín cáns.
Háve a séat by the wíndow.
She's been síck for wéeks.

### 2  — Identification —
Listen to the following sentences and write in the stress marks.
  Example:
    I cán't quíte reách it.

1. Try to reach it.
2. Tell me a story, and I'll keep still.
3. All it eats is lettuce, but it drinks a lot of gin.
4. The principal can always be reached in his office.
5. If we can't catch it we'll have to leave it behind.

**III  Intonation**

1  —  Read and Look Up  —


1. Can you see it?
2. You shouldn't bother people who are driving.
3. How many times did you have to stay after school?
4. Would you enjoy it if you had to drive a bus for a living?
5. Did you cause a lot of trouble when you were a kid?
6. Are you going to sit down or are you going to walk to school?
7. Sally tried to keep her rabbit hidden from the driver.
8. If the kids won't sit still the teacher will keep them after school.


2  —  Questions and Answers  —
Practice the questions and answers in pairs.
    Examples:

|   |   |   |   |
|---|---|---|---|
| T | feel better today | S1 | Are you feeling better today? |
|   |   | S2 | (I haven't even been sick!) |
|   | able to keep a secret | S2 | Are you able to keep a secret? |
|   |   | S3 | (No, I always tell.) |

like to live in a dormitory
keep a pet
(what) feed to a (dog) (cat) (pig), etc.
(how many times) bitten by an animal
(where) buy an animal
(where) keep goldfish
(what name) give to a (dog) (cat)
(how much) pay for a pet
(what) favorite animal


3  —  Dialog  —
Listen to the following dialog and answer the questions at the end.


On the School Bus


   Sally:  Good Morning, Mr. Crosby.
   Richard:  Good Morning, Sally. Hurry up now. Get yourself a seat. What's in the box?
   Sally:  Nothing, Mr. Crosby.
   Richard:  OK, kids, everybody sit down. Billy, get up off the floor please so we can go.
5      Sally, you can't sit up here. Go sit by the window like a good girl . . . OK. Off we go, now.
   Roger:  Mr. Crosby?
   Richard:  What?
   Roger:  Mr. Crosby?
   Richard:  What!
10   Roger:  Will you tell us a story?
   Richard:  No, Roger, I won't tell you a story. You shouldn't bother people when they're
       driving. Besides I don't know any stories.

Billy:  Mr. Crosby?

Richard:  Billy, you go back and sit down. You have to stay in your seat while the bus is
15       moving.

Billy:  Would you stop the bus, please?

Richard:  Oh, no, Billy, can't you wait till you get to school?

Billy:  No, it's not that!

Richard:  A hijacking?

20   Billy:  No, sir. Sally lost her rabbit. It jumped out of the window.

Richard:  What rabbit? What was she doing with a rabbit? Listen you kids, this bus is not
         moving until you settle down. Now what rabbit?

Billy:  Her sister's rabbit. For school. It jumped out of the box and now Sally's crying
         and she wants it back.

25   Richard:  Sally, stop crying. Can you see your rabbit?

Sally:  It's on the lawn back there.

Richard:  Can you catch it? Is it tame?

Sally:  It's a "she." All I need to catch it is a piece of lettuce.

Richard:  Billy, take a piece of lettuce from your sandwich, OK? I'm going out too, and I want
30       you kids to keep still while we're gone. Don't make any noise or you'll scare the rabbit.

Roger:  Hey, Eddy, I dare you to pull that lever.

Eddy:  For the door you mean?

Roger:  Yeah, lock old Mr. Crosby out and we won't have to go to school.

Eddy:  I dunno. He might get pretty mad.

35   Roger:  Come on, we won't tell on you, Eddy.

Eddy:  OK, but you guys better not squeal.

Roger:  Pull it back all the way, Eddy. Good work! Now get back here quick.

Eddy:  Look, they got the rabbit already. Sit down and look like nothing happened.

Richard:  I thought I told you guys to behave yourselves. Now who shut that door? Not
40       talking, eh? Open up this door, you little monsters! Yes, Roger, that means you. Push
         that lever forward. Push it harder.

Roger:  Is that OK, Mr. Crosby?

Richard:  That's fine, Roger. Now back to your seats everybody. Let's get going or you'll
         be late for school.

45   Roger:  Will you tell us a story now, Mr. Crosby?

Richard:  No, I won't. But I'm going to tell one to your principal. So sit down and hang on
         to your rabbits.


Questions: Answer briefly and be prepared to discuss in class.

1. What is the misunderstanding that occurs when Billy says, "No, it's not that!"?
   (Line 18)
2. Is a rabbit a "she" or an "it"? Explain.
3. Are these children polite? Well-behaved? Do they behave like children in your own
   culture?

## LESSON SEVENTEEN  —  Question Tags (rising intonation)  —

### I  Review of Sound Contrasts

1  —  Recognition and Production: Repetition  —

| /θ/ | /ð/ | /s/ | /z/ |
|-----|-----|-----|-----|
| ether | either | sink | zinc |
| teeth | teethe | Sue | zoo |
| loath | loathe | racer | razor |
| thistle | this'll | prices | prizes |
| mouth | mouthe | ice | eyes |

| /f/ | /v/ | /v/ | /b/ |
|-----|-----|-----|-----|
| fan | van | van | ban |
| few | view | vote | boat |
| fine | vine | curved | curbed |
| infested | invested | marvel | marble |
| belief | believe | rove | robe |

### II  Stress

1  —  Repetition  —

fáce the fácts  
thírty-twó teéth  
raísing kíds  

a sáfe invéstment  
outvóted by the oppósition  
a fíne viéw of the báy  

Pleáse clóse your eyés.  
Príces haven't incréased since lást mónth.  
Thóse are my bróther-in-law's móther's fálse teéth.

2  —  Read and Look Up  —
Be prepared to say which words are stressed.

1. This is a fine view.
2. Don't put ice in the wine.
3. You can't shave without a razor.
4. That little boy has only three front teeth left.
5. He always believed his brother's excuses.
6. Let's vote on the proposal and discuss it afterwards.
7. She's sitting about five feet behind the bow of the boat.

this exercise continued on next page

8. Move the fan over by the bed and leave the window open.
9. They invested their money in worthless stocks.
10. Nobody thought of giving the boy a day off.


**III  Question Tags with Rising Intonation**

---

*Generalization:*  A question tag may have rising intonation just like an ordinary *Yes* / *No* question. In this case the speaker is asking for real information, but he expects the listener to agree. The answer to this kind of question tag usually takes falling intonation. Example:

Today is Monday, isn't it?  Yes, it is.

---

1  —  Positive Statement / Negative Tag: Repetition  —

| Question | Answer |
|---|---|
| 1. You're taking the test, aren't you? | Yes, I am. |
| 2. They've finished with the book, haven't they? | Yes, they have. |
| 3. You can go to the game, can't you? | Yes, I can. |
| 4. He'll have to write a paper, won't he? | Yes, he will. |

2  —  Negative Statement / Positive Tag: Repetition  —

| Question | Answer |
|---|---|
| 1. He couldn't mean that, could he? | No, he couldn't. |
| 2. They don't always go to the games, do they? | No, they don't. |
| 3. He won't bother us, will he? | No, he won't. |
| 4. You didn't forget to study for the test, did you? | No, I didn't. |

---

*Note:*  In III 1 and 2 above the listener agreed with the speaker. If, however, the listener does not agree with what he hears, he should give a brief explanation of the reasons for his disagreement. Example:

You work today, don't you?          No, not today. I have the day off.

---

3  —  Repetition  —

| Question | Answer |
|---|---|
| 1. You're taking the test, aren't you? | No, I'm not. (I took it yesterday.) |
| 2. You can go to the game, can't you? | No, I can't. (I don't have any money.) |
| 3. He couldn't mean that, could he? | Yes, he could. (He was very angry.) |
| 4. He's not giving a speech today, is he? | Yes, he is. (You know how he loves to talk.) |

4 — Question Tag and Disagreement (Negative Tag) —
Examples:

|  |  |  |  |
|---|---|---|---|
| T | you / like baseball | S1 | You like baseball, don't you? |
|  |  | S2 | No, I don't. (I can't understand it at all.) |
|  | (José) / can swim | S2 | José can swim, can't he? |
|  |  | S3 | No, he can't. (He never learned how.) |

you / enjoy music
(Mohammed) / give a good speech
you / graduate this year
Language Lab / closed tomorrow
(Pradit) / have a part-time job
your advisor / have an office in (Bruce) Hall
you / should stop (smoking)
(Miguel) / passed the TOEFL test

5 — Question Tag and Disagreement (Positive Tag) —
Examples:

|  |  |  |  |
|---|---|---|---|
| T | you / quit school | S1 | You're not quitting school, are you? |
|  |  | S2 | Yes, I am. (I think I've learned enough.) |
|  | (José) / play chess | S2 | José can't play chess, can he? |
|  |  | S3 | Yes, he can. (He's the best player in the class.) |

you / come from (Egypt)
(Miguel) / spend a lot of time in the library
you / smoke cigars
(Mohammed) / drive a car to school
you / finish research paper
(José) / live in an apartment
you / read mystery novels
you / know how to type
you / return home next month

> *Note:* Sometimes words like *OK, right,* and *all right* are used as question tags and take rising intonation. Examples:
>     You live in Oakland, right?  (speaker asks for agreement)
>     Sit in the front row, OK?  (polite request)
>     Do this homework for tomorrow, all right?  (polite command)

6 — Practice: Question and Answer —
Examples:

|  |  |  |  |
|---|---|---|---|
| T | you / like baseball | S1 | You like baseball, don't you? |
|  |  | S2 | Yes, I do. (No, I don't.) |
|  |  | S1 | Why? (Why not?) |
|  |  | S2 | It's exciting. (It's boring.) |

this exercise continued on next page

T        (José) / quit school

S2    José didn't quit sch\ool, did ⌐he?
S3    No, he did\n't. (Yes, he did.)
S2    Why no\t? (Why?)
S3    He wants a deg\ree. (He got a job.)

you / swim the English Channel
(Mohammed) / talk with his advisor
you / own a television
(José) / sell his car
you / run for President
(Rafael) / go to New York for the weekend
you / feel well today
(Pradit) / like to play basketball
you / refuse a job with the government
you / lend me $5000.00

7  —  Dialog  —
Listen to the following dialog and answer the questions at the end.

At the Department Library

Miguel:  Arnold, you're taking Lurch's test tomorrow, aren't you?
Arnold:  Uh-huh. And I haven't done any of the reading yet. You've finished with this
         journal, haven't you, Pat?
Pat:  Sure, go ahead. Oh, Arnold, I forgot to tell you. A group of us are going to the
5        basketball game Friday night, and I wanted to ask you to go too. You like
         basketball, don't you?
Arnold:  I don't know. I don't think I've ever played.
Miguel:  What? Arnold, you did have a childhood, didn't you?
Arnold:  A very brief one. I remember I learned to play the violin. My mother . . .
10   Pat:  I know. Your mother says you have talent. But not in basketball, right? Well,
         you don't have to play, just watch. A lot of us are going together. Dick Crosby
         is getting tickets so we want to know for sure how many people are going.
Arnold: Crosby isn't going is he? How does that guy find the time—and money?
         Pat, I don't know about this Friday. I've got to be at work early Saturday
15       morning, and I haven't even begun my paper for Dr. Lurchmint.
Miguel:  Speak of the devil! That's him coming now, isn't it?
Pat:  Oh, no! Quick, look busy and maybe he won't bother us.
Lurchmint:  Good afternoon, gentlemen and lady. Preparing for the test, are we?
         Fine, but I'm sure you're aware of my public imprecations against this last
20       minute cramming, right? That's my article you're reading, isn't it, Bixby?
Arnold:  Yes, sir. I was just looking it over one last time before the test.
Lurchmint:  Good, excellent. Oh, before you go, Bixby, would you stop by my
         office for a moment please. I've just finished a chapter that you might be
         interested in perusing.
25   Arnold:  Oh, yes, sir. I'll be right with you.
Miguel:  You have my sympathies, Arnold. When Lurch starts talking, you'll be
         listening to his "public imprecations" for hours.
Pat:  That is, when you're not "perusing" the latest chapter in his latest book.
Arnold:  I don't see what you're complaining about. I consider it a pleasure to
30       talk with a real professional like Lurchmint.

Pat:  Oh, Arnold, you don't mean that, do you? Lurch is such an awful bore.

Arnold:  Of course I mean it. I think Lurchmint is a great man. Talking to him
is certainly more valuable than watching a basketball game, don't you think?
At least some people are more interested in research than in watching men
35      throw a ball around in the air.

Miguel:  He doesn't mean that, does he? Nobody could hate basketball so much.

Pat:  Oh, he doesn't hate basketball. He just thinks he should be doing great things
and we don't do great things.

Miguel:  And Lurch does?

40   Pat:  It's hard to imagine. You don't think he could be right, do you?

Miguel:  Don't worry. I've never known Arnold to be right about anything.


Questions: Answer briefly and be prepared to discuss in class.

1. How do Pat and Miguel feel about Dr. Lurchmint? How do they express their feelings?
2. How does Arnold feel about Dr. Lurchmint and how does he express his feeling?
3. How would you react in a similar situation? Would you rather spend time talking to
   professors or watching a basketball game? Explain.

# LESSON EIGHTEEN — /e/ and /ey/ —

## I Recognition and Production

### 1 — Repetition —

| /e/ | /ey/ | | /e/ | /ey/ |
|-----|------|---|-----|------|
| rest | raced | | test | taste |
| edge | age | | west | waste |
| sell | sale | | fell | fail |
| debt | date | | bet | bait |
| get | gate | | wet | wait |

## II Stress

### 1 — Repetition —

what a sháme!
a tále to téll
máke a bét
páy the rént
for héaven's sáke
sáve the rést

a táste test
máke a dáte
a chéss player
gét a héadache
paínt the dén
táke a pláne

### 2 — Identification —

Write in the stress marks for the following sentences. Your teacher will not say them until you are finished. Be prepared to read the sentences aloud.

Example:

They dón't báke bréad on Wédnesdays.

1. Haste makes waste.
2. Save the rest for later.
3. Let's make it a date.
4. Don't forget to pay the rent.
5. You can place bets at the horse races.

## III  Intonation

1  —  Read and Look Up  —
Be prepared to identify intonation patterns.

1. Chess players often get headaches.
2. How much will you bet he fails the test?
3. They'll be here before eight, won't they?
4. Taste it first, then tell us how you like it.
5. If you have to take the test, don't be late for it.
6. For heaven's sakes, they can take a plane, can't they?
7. Mayors hardly ever make mistakes, right?
8. If I'm not mistaken the eight o'clock train has already left.
9. They complained about having no place to go to play chess.
10. What a shame that they can't take the train instead.

2  —  Practice:  Telephone Questions and Requests  —
Suppose that you are an instructor of a class in "How to Play Golf." Some of your students call in with questions and requests concerning the course. Answer the question or request and give a reason for your response.

Example:

| S1 | (on the telephone) Excuse me, Mr. (Gomez), do you mind if I come late to class on Wednesdays? I have to take my children to school that morning. | S2 | I'm sorry, Mr. (Lopez), but if you're late, you'll miss the bus to the golf course. (or: Well, all right. But try to come as early as possible.) |

| S1 | telephones | S2 | to ask if it's all right to come to class an hour late every day. |
| S2 | telephones | S3 | to ask if he has to buy golf clubs for the course. |
| S3 | telephones | S4 | to ask if he can still get into the course even though instruction began a week ago. |
| | | | to ask if he has to pay or if the course is free. |
| | | | to ask if you need an assistant instructor for the course. |
| | | | to ask if he will learn well enough to play as a professional. |
| | | | to ask if a person who has never played before can enroll in the course. |
| | | | to ask if there is a penalty for registering late. |
| | | | to ask if there are any good-looking women (men) in the class. |
| | | | to ask if he can wait to pay tuition until next Spring. |
| | | | to ask if it is all right to wear jeans and tennis shoes to the graduation ceremony. |

3 — Dialog —
Listen to the dialog and answer the questions at the end. Harriet is giving Yoga lessons in her home.

## HARRIET'S HOUSE OF YOGA

Mrs. Terrill: Harriet, I hope you can do something for me. My husband said I look like a
potato.

Harriet: What an awful thing to say, Mrs. Terrill.

Mrs. Terrill: Believe me, the little jerk is sorry he said it. He suffered for that remark. But the
5    really awful thing is that it's true. I even feel like a potato!

Harriet: Nonsense! The first thing you have to learn is how to relax. Ladies, all of you, please
lie down and relax for the first five minutes. We can't begin any exercises until you're all
relaxed.

Mrs. Mortenson: Is it all right, Harriet, if we bring pillows to class? This floor is so hard!

10    Harriet: No, Mrs. Mortenson, no pillows please. We don't want you to fall asleep. And Mrs.
Mortenson, please, you mustn't wear tennis shoes when you practice Yoga. Barefeet
only, please.

Anne: Harriet! Telephone!

Harriet: What do they want?

15    Anne: I don't know. Somebody who wants to "consult Mrs. Crosby personally."

Harriet: OK. Will you take over, Anne? Relax now. Breathe slowly . . . deeply. I'll be back in
a second . . . Hello?

Mrs. Lurchmint: Hello? Harriet Crosby?

Harriet: Yes, may I help you?

15    Mrs. Lurchmint: My dear Mrs. Crosby, this is Bosworthia Lurchmint calling. Forgive me for
interrupting you, but I did so want to talk to you directly.

Harriet: Certainly, Mrs. Lurchmint. What can I do for you?

Mrs. Lurchmint: I would like to inquire about your class for beginners.

Harriet: But you talked with my assistant. Surely she told you that the course is already
20    overcrowded. And we've been holding classes for over a week.

Mrs. Lurchmint: Yes, of course I spoke with your very capable assistant, and she was kind
enough to take my name and number. But I was hoping that you personally might see
fit to make the tiniest exception in my case. I was looking forward to this course so much.

Harriet: I wish I could help you. But the class is already so large, and I have only one
25    assistant. I couldn't possibly take any more students at this time. There will, however,
be another class in the Spring.

Mrs. Lurchmint: I see. In the Spring. Well, if there is nothing you can do. But my husband
did recommend you so highly. You are acquainted with my husband?

Harriet: I don't believe so. But I assure you I'll keep your name and number, and you'll be
30    the first to know when a new class forms.

Mrs. Lurchmint: Well, all right. Thank you. Good-bye, Mrs. Crosby.

Harriet: Good-bye. . . . Lurchmint? You don't suppose it could be . . .

Anne: Harriet, it's time to go. They're getting restless out there.

Harriet: Anne, I'm afraid that woman I was just talking to is *somebody*.

35    Anne: I'm sure she is, Harriet. But let's get to work.

Harriet: Oh, no. I think I've just ruined my husband's career.

Anne: Believe me, that would be no great loss. Now let's go!

**this exercise continued on next page**

Questions:

1. Why does Mrs. Lurchmint insist on speaking to Harriet directly?
2. Mrs. Lurchmint makes a "polite" request. How is the "politeness" expressed?
3. At the end why is Harriet worried?

# LESSON NINETEEN — Falling Intonation in Question Tags —

## I Review of /i/, /iy/ and /e/, /ey/

### 1 — Repetition —

| /i/ | /iy/ | | /e/ | /ey/ |
|------|-------|---|------|-------|
| sit | seat | | tell | tail |
| fit | feet | | test | taste |
| still | steal | | fell | fail |
| will | we'll | | edge | age |
| it | eat | | sell | sale |
| hit | heat | | debt | date |
| slip | sleep | | get | gate |
| sick | seek | | west | waste |

### 2 — Recognition —

Listen to the following sentences. If the word you hear in the blank has the /i/ sound, say 1; if it has the /iy/ sound, say 2.

Example:

    T  She tried to *heat* it.          S  2.

             1    2

1. She tried to *(hit)* *(heat)* it.
2. You'll have to *(slip)* *(sleep)* it off.
3. I don't know what *(will)* *(we'll)* do.
4. *(His)* *(He's)* home.
5. We forced him to *(it)* *(eat)*.
6. I *(still)* *(steal)* like my brother.

If the word you hear has the /e/ sound, say 1: if it has the /ey/ sound, say 2.

             1     2

1. The police are *(telling)* *(tailing)* me.
2. It depends on what kind of *(test)* *(taste)* you have.
3. I don't want to know if they *(fell)* *(fail)*.
4. It's best to forget about old *(debts)* *(dates)*.
5. The *(edge)* *(age)* of the table was remarkable.

## II   Falling Intonation in Question Tags

---

*Generalization:*  Falling intonation on a question tag usually indicates that the speaker is not really seeking new information. Rather the speaker intends for the listener to agree. Example:

Nice day, isn't it?                    Yes, it is.

---

1 — Practice:  Positive Statement / Negative Tag: Repetition —

| Question | Answer |
|---|---|
| 1. You really like soccer don't you? | Yes, I do. |
| 2. He's pretty smart, isn't he? | Yes, he is. |
| 3. She's left already, hasn't she? | Yes, she has. |
| 4. They can read Arabic, can't they? | Yes, they can. |
| 5. We're out of time, aren't we? | Yes, we are. |

2 — Practice:  Negative Statement / Positive Tag: Repetition —

| Question | Answer |
|---|---|
| 1. You don't believe me, do you? | No, I don't. |
| 2. You two haven't met yet, have you? | No, we haven't. |
| 3. There isn't any time left, is there? | No, there isn't. |
| 4. They won't finish on time, will they? | No, they won't. |
| 5. She never did write to us, did she? | No, she didn't. |

---

*Note:*  A question tag with falling intonation may compel the listener to disagree with the speaker because he doesn't like or agree with what the speaker says. When disagreeing one should give a reason or excuse. Example:

You won't be finished on time, will you?      Well of course I will! I always finish my work on time.

---

3 — Practice:  Disagreement: Repetition —

1. You're not very good in math, are you?        Yes, I am! I always get good grades in math.
2. You don't like me, do you?        Of course I do! I've known you for years.
3. Arnold isn't very bright, is he?        Oh, I think he must be. He always gets good grades.
4. You haven't met her yet, have you?        Oh, yes. We met at the party.

4 — Practice: Disagreement (Negative Statement / Positive Tags)  —
Examples:

  T    (Pradit) / fail the test        S1    Pradit didn't fail the te\st, did⌐ he?
                                       S2    Yes, he di⌐d! (He got only two correct.)

       you / know French               S2    You don't know Fre⌐nch, do⌐ you?
                                       S3    But I d⌐o! (I used to live in France.)

  (Mohammed) / live in Italy
  you / go downtown
  (José) / finish homework
  you / write a book
  (Miguel) / arrive on time
  you / believe in ghosts
  (Ali) / have enough money
  you / read Chinese
  (Amir) / like hamburgers
  you / eat breakfast
  (Carlos) / type 50 words a minute
  you / remember to mail the letter
  (Abdul) / quit school


5 — Disagreement (Positive Statement / Negative Tag)  —
Examples:

  T    (Abdul) / tired                 S1    Abdul is pretty ti\red, isn't\ he?
                                       S2    No\. (He hasn't done anything at all today.)

       you / can type                  S2    You can ty\pe, can't\ you?
                                       S3    No\. (I always pay someone to type my papers for
                                             me.)

  (Miguel) / come to class
  you / can swim pretty fast
  (José) / leave for home
  you / too old to play tennis
  (Talib) / finish homework early
  you / accept the job in Chicago
  (Carlos) / play the piano well
  you / like to go to the opera
  (Amir) / study Spanish
  you / come late
  (Preecha) / live in a dorm
  you / pay tuition
  (Ali) / move to New York


6 — Practice: Question with Falling Intonation Tag Followed by Disagreement  —
Examples:

  T    (Miguel) / go downtown          S1    Miguel isn't going downtown\tomorrow, is\ he?
                                       S2    Sure he is. (He has to buy a birthday present for
                                             Ali.)


this exercise continued on next page

you / take test

S2   You're taking the t̄est\tomorrow, aren͡t\you?

S3   No! (I'm writing a paper instead.)

(Gonzalo) / going home tomorrow

you / want to get a driver's license

(          ) / need a new watch

you / go to Los Angeles

(          ) / read Chinese

you / sleep in the Language Lab

(          ) / study engineering

you / would like a part-time job

(          ) / take the bus to school

you / spend your vacation in Canada next year

(          ) / apply for a job in Chicago

you / skip lunch today

(          ) / enjoy water skiing

you / write a book


7  — Dialog —

Listen to the following dialog and answer the questions at the end.


### Arnold Goes to Work


Mrs. Bixby:  Arnold! Hurry up or you'll be late for work!

Arnold:  Be right there. I'm on my way. Oh, Lord, it couldn't be morning already. You
don't really want to get up, do you, Arnold? No, I don't. It's too early, isn't it? Yes,
it is. But we have to, don't we? Oh, shut up.

5    Mrs. Bixby:  Arnold, stop mumbling and come down here. Drink your coffee, dear.

Arnold:  What coffee?

Mrs. Bixby:  It's right in front of you! You were up studying all night again, weren't you?

Arnold:  Not all night, mother.

Mrs. Bixby:  Well, you need your rest too, you know. Today's a work day for you. Arnold!

10    What kind of chemist are you? You're putting salt in your coffee.

Arnold:  Oops!

Mrs. Bixby:  Salt on your eggs, dear. Sugar in the coffee.

Arnold:  Thank you, mother. I'm going to be late this evening. I have to go to the lab after
work.

15    Mrs. Bixby:  Arnold, you're never here in the evenings. And you never play for us any more.
There's no music in this house.

Arnold:  I've got to work at this crummy job. I've got no time.

Mrs. Bixby:  It's not a crummy job. You should be grateful to Richard for helping you find it.
Especially under the circumstances.

20    Beth:  Yeah, you should be grateful. Because otherwise you wouldn't have the money to go to
school, would you?

Arnold:  My poor misinformed little sister. If you don't mind . . .

Mrs. Bixby:  Beth, be still.

Beth:  Oh, Mom, he's just a sorehead because he didn't get his ridiculous "scholarship."

25    Arnold:  "Fellowship." And that's not true!

Mrs. Bixby:  Beth, run along to school, dear.

Beth:  But, Mom, today's Saturday.

Arnold:  Run along anyway. Pretend it's Monday. I should be grateful for that crummy job?

Mrs. Bixby:  What will you be doing at work today, dear?

30 Arnold:  Same as always. I mix cement. Gus stops by and says, "Cold out today, ain't it?" Then old Steve comes over to watch and says, "You sure don't know much about cement, do you?" Today if he says that, he's going to fall into the mixing machine.

Mrs. Bixby:  Arnold, that kind of talk won't do any good now, will it? You should relax more. Whatever happened to that nice girl Pat . . . what's her name? Why don't you go out with

35 her anymore?

Arnold:  Mother, I don't have time to tie my shoelaces!

Mrs. Bixby:  No excuses, please. And another thing, Arnold. You owe Richard Crosby a favor. Why don't you help him out with his research project?

Arnold:  We are working along the same lines, that's true.

40 Mrs. Bixby:  So you will help him, won't you? He's such a nice boy.

Arnold:  Maybe I should invite him over to the job site. Then he could accidentally fall into the cement mixer. Along with old Steve. I'll mix them both into a big cement ball and roll it into the Atlantic Ocean.

Mrs. Bixby:  You're never serious for a minute, are you, dear?

45 Arnold:  Mother, I promise you I'll see what I can do for our old friend, Dick Crosby.


Questions:

1. Why does Arnold dislike "old Steve?"
2. What's your opinion of Mrs. Bixby?
3. Is Arnold going to "help" Dick Crosby?

# LESSON TWENTY -- /u/ and /uw/

## I Recognition and Production

### 1 — Repetition —

| /u/ | /uw/ |
|-----|------|
| full | fool |
| could | cooed |
| look | Luke |
| should | shoed |
| pull | pool |
| would | wooed |

## II Stress

### 1 — Repetition —

a héated póol

in a góod móod

óff the hóok

Ópen your bóoks please.

Are you chéwing your fóod?

Whóse bóok is this?

You've got nóthing to lóse.

the wáter cooler

a rúde awákening

a úsed cóokbook

### 2 — Read and Look Up.
Be prepared to identify stressed syllables.

1. You haven't got anything to lose, have you?
2. We took off our shoes and jumped into the pool.
3. I think the blue one would look good on you.
4. Are you through looking?
5. We took a good look at the book before we put it back.
6. If you're not in a good mood, you should go out and buy a new pair of shoes.
7. Whose book are you looking at?
8. Is it true that you used glue to put the book back together?
9. Would you open your books to page twenty-two, please?

## III  Intonation

1  —  Review of Tag Questions: Repetition  —

| Question | Answer |
|---|---|

1. You're a good co͡o͡k, aren't you?  Yes, I am.
2. You didn't say anything rude to Bud, did you?  No, but I would have if I hadn't been in such a good mood.
3. Do you mean he refuses to wear shoes to school?  That's what they say, but it couldn't be true, could it?
4. May I take a look at your book?  You really shouldn't since the language is rather crude.
5. You put something in the orange juice, didn't you?  Well, yes, I threw in a few prunes and a cookie.

2  —  Polite Requests  —

Suppose that you are an advisor to students and have to answer their questions and requests.

---

*Note:* Polite requests often take rising intonation. Remember that if you refuse a request, you should explain *why* you have to refuse.

---

Examples:

| | | |
|---|---|---|
| T | give me an appointment for next Monday | S1 | Could you give me an appointment for next Monday, please? |
| | | S2 | Yes, of course. Come in any time. (No, I'm sorry. I'll be out of town all next week.) |
| | write a recommendation for me | S2 | Would you write a recommendation for me, please? |
| | | S3 | Sure, I'll be glad to. (I would like to, but I'm really not familiar with your academic work.) |

speak at our foreign students' dinner
show me where the book store is
help me fill out a registration form
translate this letter (for me)
lend me some money until the first of the month
show me how to do a problem in statistics
vote for me in the Student Council Election
come to  a party at my apartment this Saturday
proofread my research paper
lend me your library card
help me write a letter to graduate school
tell me where the post office is

this exercise continued on next page

explain how I can extend my visa
sign my registration form
lend me money for bus fare
tell me how to find the Student Health Center

3   —   Dialog   —
Listen to the following dialog and answer the questions at the end.


At the Department

Pat:  Dick! When did you sneak in here? You scared me to death!
Richard:  Sh!!
Pat:  What's the matter with you?
Richard:  I came here to get some books, but I don't want Lurch to see me.
5   Pat:  Why not?
Richard:  I'm afraid he may ask me about my research project. I haven't
      even written the proposal yet.
Pat:  But Dick, the project is due at the end of the month!
Richard:  I know, I know. I wish I could forget.
10  Pat:  Dick, look out! Here he comes!
Richard:  Lurch? Oh, God, I'm sunk. Pat, go out and try to distract him, will you?
Pat:  I can't. I'd feel so ridiculous.
Lurchmint:  What's "so ridiculous"? Ah, Richard, what a rare pleasure to see you in our
      library.
15  Richard:  Well, I . . . I . . . I . . . I . . . I . . . spend a lot of time in the laboratory. I was just on
      my way to work, and I thought I'd stop by to look up a few sources for my research
      project.
Lurchmint:  Oh, that reminds me. I wonder if I could speak to you in my office for a few
      minutes. You do have time, don't you?
20  Richard:  Oh, yes, of course. I'll be right with you . . . This looks like the end, Pat. It's
      been nice knowing you.
Pat:  You can't run away now, Dick. Go see what he wants. Maybe it's nothing. Well, go on,
      silly!
Lurchmint:  Ah, come on in and sit down, Richard. Make yourself at home. I'm afraid that
25     what I want to talk to you about is rather personal.
Richard:  If it's about my grades, sir, I want you to know that I'm not at all satisfied with the
      work I've done so far. I can do better.
Lurchmint:  Oh, yes, grades. Very important of course. But, actually, that's not what I called
      you in here to talk about. I'd like to ask you a little favor. You see, my wife is interested
30     in that exercise class that your wife teaches . . .
Richard:  Harriet's Yoga course?
Lurchmint:  Precisely. My wife is very eager to enroll in the beginning class.
Richard:  I'm sure that Harriet would be delighted to have her.
Lurchmint:  Yes, indeed. But there seems to be a slight problem, Richard. My wife has
35     spoken to Harriet, but the class seems to be full. Needless to say Bosworthia was very
      disappointed.
Richard:  Dr. Lurchmint, I'm sure something can be done. There must have been a
      misunderstanding of some kind. I know Harriet will be glad to have your wife enroll
      when she realizes how important it is—to your wife I mean.

40    Lurchmint:  Well, fine, fine, Richard. That's good news. I can count on hearing from you
         soon then?
      Richard:  I'll let you know tonight. Or Harriet may wish to call your wife directly.
      Lurchmint:  Excellent! And about those grades of yours, Richard. I wouldn't worry too much
         about them now. Do a real knockout job on your final project and I won't pay much
45       attention to your earlier work.
      Richard:  Thank you very much, Dr. Lurchmint. May I stop by again to discuss my research
         project with you?
      Lurchmint:  Any time, Richard, any time.


Questions:

1. When speaking to Dr. Lurchmint, why does Richard say "I . . . I . . . I . . . I . . . I"?
   Isn't one pronoun enough?
2. Was there really a "misunderstanding"? If not, why does Richard say there was?
3. Why would Harriet "wish to" call Bosworthia Lurchmint directly?

**LESSON TWENTY ONE — Falling Intonation in Special Emphasis —**

**I Production**

> *Generalization:* Intonation in a statement usually falls at the end of the sentence. If, however, the speaker emphasizes a word earlier in the utterance, that word is heavily stressed. The intonation falls at that point of emphasis and stays down.
>     Example   (Normal Intonation):
>
>         He's got to drive his uncle's car to Chica go.
>
> a. Special Emphasis on *car:*
>    He's got to drive his uncle's *car* to Chicago.          (*car,* not his uncle's motorcycle)
> b. Special Emphasis on *uncle's:*
>    He's got to drive his *uncle's* car to Chicago.          (his *uncle's,* not his brother's car)
> c. Special Emphasis on *has got to:*
>    He's *got* to drive his uncle's car to Chicago.          (He *must* do it; he has no choice.)
> d. Special Emphasis on *He:*
>    *He's* got to drive his uncle's car to Chicago.          (*He,* not somebody else)

1 — Repetition —

1. We're going to Pittsburgh next we ek.
2. We're going to Pittsburgh *next* week.
3. We're going to *Pitts burgh* next week.
4. *We're* going to Pittsburgh next week.

2 — Practice —
Listen and repeat the following sentence; then say the sentence again applying special emphasis to the cue word.

1. They always refused to speak to us in En glish.

| T | *us*     | S1 | They always refused to speak to *us* in English. |
|   | *speak*  | S2 | They always refused to *speak* to us in English. |
|   | *always* | S3 |   |
|   | *They*   | S4 |   |

2. I would like to move to Arizona next September.

| T | *next*    |
|   | *Arizona* |
|   | *I*       |

3. She finished writing her French composition after mid night.

| T | *after*       |
|   | *composition* |
|   | *French*      |
|   | *writing*     |
|   | *She*         |

this exercise continued on next page

4. He said that no one in his psychology class completed the paper on ti\me.

T   *paper*
    *completed*
    *psychology*
    *his*
    *no one*
    *He*

## II   Identification and Practice

1  —  Practice  —

Listen and repeat the following sentences; then apply special emphasis to the cue words. When you answer questions, *deny* the point that is emphasized.

1. You didn't eat that water\melon, did/you? (normal intonation)

T   *eat*        S1   You didn't *eat*\that watermelon, did/you?
                 S2   No! (I put it in the refrigerator.)
    *that*       S2   You didn't eat *that*\watermelon, did/you?
                 S3   No. (I ate the other one.)
    *You*        S3   *You*\didn't eat that watermelon, did/you?
                 S4   No, not me! (Arnold ate it.)

2. They haven't finished their research for Dr. Lurch\mint, have/they?

T   *research*
    *finished*
    *They*

3. She ate two dozen bananas with her lunch\today, didn't\she?

T   *bananas*
    *dozen*
    *two*

4. Richard would like to raise a dog in his apar\tment, wouldn't/he?

T   *his*
    *dog*
    *like*
    *Richard*

5. Harriet hates to eat toast for break\fast, doesn't\she?

T   *toast*
    *hates*
    *Harriet*

6. Arnold threw his old typewriter into the garbage\can, didn't\he?

T   *typewriter*
    *old*
    *his*
    *Arnold*

*Note:* Sometimes special emphasis may be placed on two (or more) items in a sentence. In this case stress and intonation fall on *each* instance of special emphasis. This often occurs when two surprising items are mentioned together. Examples:

Richard wouldn't eat *alligator* meat for *dinner*, would he?

You don't eat *cookies* with your *orange juice*, do you?

2 — Practice: Repetition —

1. You wouldn't mix *cookies* in your *salad*, would you?
2. You don't keep *alligators* in your *house*, do you?
3. They wouldn't invite *Arnold* to the *party*, would they?
4. She hasn't put *salt* in the *lemonade*, has she?

3 — Practice: Double Emphasis —
Example:

| T | gorilla / kitchen | S1 | You wouldn't keep a *gorilla* in your *kitchen*, would you? |
| | | S2 | No! (I would never keep any pets in the kitchen.) |
| | carrots / snadwiches | S2 | You don't put *carrots* in your *sandwiches*, do you? |
| | | S3 | No. (I prefer lettuce in my sandwiches.) |

glue / salad
rhinoceros / garage
telephone / closet
cobra / refrigerator
ice cubes / soup
lemon / cookies
television / bathroom

3 — Dialog —
Listen to the following dialog and answer the questions at the end.

Birthday Shopping

Robert: I don't see why you need me to tag along, Harriet. You've got the car today, you could pick it up yourself.

Harriet: Oh, I may need some help with it. I didn't take you away from anything important this afternoon, did I?

5 Robert: No, no. I'm just curious, that's all. I wonder why you need *my* help to pick up a birthday present for Dick. Must be a big gift.

Harriet: Yeah, pretty big.

Robert: Heavy?

Harriet: Mm-hm.

10   Robert:  Well?
     Harriet:  Well what?
     Robert:  Well, what is it?
     Harriet:  Bob, I shouldn't tell you yet. It's a surprise.
     Robert:  But it's not *my* birthday! You can tell *me.*
15   Harriet:  Well, if you promise to do me a little favor.
     Robert:  What kind of favor?
     Harriet:  Keep the present at your apartment until the party.
     Robert:  What's the matter? Why can't *you* keep it at *your* apartment?
     Harriet:  I don't think I could hide it from Dick.
20   Robert:  What in the world is it, Harriet?
     Harriet:  Do you promise?
     Robert:  This is ridiculous! What are you trying to make me promise?
     Harriet:  We'd better stop here.
     Robert:  Why? What now?
25   Harriet:  We're just about there. Bob, can't you do me this little favor? It's only for a couple
         of days, after all. I promise you it won't cause you any trouble or cost you any money.
     Robert:  Harriet, why are we stopped here anyway? There are no department stores on this
         block. Wait a minute . . . It's that pet store over there, isn't it?
     Harriet:  Bob, promise you'll keep it.
30   Robert:  I see what you're up to. You're going to buy a rhinoceros or a gorilla or something
         for Dick's birthday, and you want *me* to keep it, right?
     Harriet:  It's not a gorilla, Bob. It's just a little dog.
     Robert:  I *knew* it. I knew there was something fishy about all this. Harriet, I can't *keep*
         pets at my apartment. And I *hate* dogs.
35   Harriet:  Well, it's not *your* pet. And you'll *love* this dog. He's a sweet little puppy. Only
         eleven weeks old.
     Robert:  A dirty little mutt! I won't do it.
     Harriet:  Only for a couple of days. How can I keep him at *our* place?
     Robert:  Why couldn't you just buy Dick a monopoly game or an electric toothbrush?
40       Something practical.
     Harriet:  He *likes* dogs. *I* like dogs. *Everybody* likes dogs. What's the matter with *you?*
     Robert:  All right, all right. I'll do it. I'll put up with it. Just don't tell me again that
         it's a "sweet little puppy." And *you* provide the dog food, all right?
     Harriet:  All right.


Questions:

1. What's the difference between a "dirty little mutt" and a "sweet little puppy"?
2. How does the stress or intonation show that Robert is upset?
3. In your country would you buy an animal for a gift? Explain.

# LESSON TWENTY-TWO — /l/ and /r/ —

## I Recognition and Production

### 1 — Repetition —

| | | | | | |
|---|---|---|---|---|---|
| late | rate | cloud | crowd | tile | tire |
| law | raw | flee | free | role | roar |
| lead | read | rolling | roaring | stole | store |
| lice | rice | miller | mirror | coal | core |
| light | right | glass | grass | steal | steer |
| lock | rock | collect | correct | dial | dire |
| low | row | files | fires | file | fire |
| long | wrong | believed | bereaved | wall | war |

### 2 — Identification —

Listen to your teacher read the following sentences. If the word in the blank has the /l/ sound, say 1; if it has the /r/ sound, say 2.

Example:

T    We couldn't move the *rock*.          S  2.

                            1    2

1. We couldn't move the *(lock) (rock)*.
2. She gave us the *(long) (wrong)* one.
3. The king refused to *(flee) (free)* the city.
4. He disappeared into the *(cloud) (crowd)*.
5. We walked barefoot on the *(glass) (grass)*.
6. *(Collect) (correct)* the papers please.
7. She found some *(lice) (rice)* in his hair.
8. He put it in the *(file) (fire)*.

## II Stress

### 1 — Repetition —

| | |
|---|---|
| lóts of lúck | flý nów, páy láter |
| róck 'n róll | fréezing cóld |
| a stólen cár | bróken gláss |
| ríght and wróng | a róaring fíre |
| véry crówded | láw and órder |

Colléct the pápers.
He presénted the bíll.
We had a flát tíre.
Máke a ríght túrn at the córner.

2  —  Read and Look Up.

Be prepared to identify stressed syllables.

1. The car had a flat tire on the freeway.
2. Be sure to make a right turn at the freeway.
3. I wish you lots of luck in tomorrow's race.
4. Collect the papers after class and give them to the teacher for correcting.
5. The "Fly now, pay later" plan doesn't really allow you a free holiday.
6. Pat's paragraph is correct, but Arnold will have to write his over.
7. Every winter they go swimming in the frozen water of the lake.
8. The waiter presented the bill after dinner, but Harriet refused to pay it.
9. He was so tired that he fell asleep during the final exam.
10. Just after the Christmas holidays the department store had to close for repairs.

## III   Intonation

1  —  Review of Tag Questions: Repetition  —

| Question | Answer |
|---|---|
| 1. We turn right here, don't we? | No, no. We go left at every corner. |
| 2. We turn right here, don't we? | No, no, it's the next corner. |
| 3. Do we have any beer in the refrigerator? | No, you drank it all up. |
| 4. Where's the nearest bowling alley? | There's one down the street, but it's always crowded. |
| 5. You drove to the store this morning, didn't you? | No, we'll have to go tonight. |

2  —  Practice: Misunderstanding  —

Read the sentences to yourself. Then look up and say them aloud selecting the word in parentheses that is more appropriate. Then in response to the teacher's question repeat the sentence giving special emphasis to the appropriate word.

Examples:

S1   We always *(fly) (fry)* our eggs for breakfast.
T    Do you say *fly* or *fry*?          S1    We always *fry* our eggs for breakfast.
S2   We *(locked) (rocked)* the door behind us when we left.
T    Do you say *locked* or *rocked*?    S2    We *locked* the door behind us when we left.
S3   She had the best *(role) (roar)* in the play.
T    Do you say *role* or *roar*?        S3    She had the best *role* in the play.

1. Without civil *(lights) (rights)* you can't enjoy life very much.
2. One of the *(tiles) (tires)* fell off when we stopped the car.
3. We *(collect) (correct)* stamps from all countries as a hobby.
4. He turned on the *(lights) (rights)* when he drove through the tunnel.
5. The *(laughter) (rafter)* of the theater is really the best part.
6. The big *(clouds) (crowds)* in New York make it difficult to go shopping.

**this exercise continued on next page**

 7. We had to *(flee) (free)* the country after robbing the bank.
 8. The doctor discovered *(lice) (rice)* in the men's hair.
 9. He was never able to *(steal) (steer)* the car in a straight line.
10. The *(glass) (grass)* she was drinking from was green.


3  —  Dialog  —

Listen to the following dialog and answer the questions at the end.


### The Formal Dinner

Pat:  Rotl who?

Arnold:  Tosca! Rotl Tosca. I'm surprised at you, Pat. He's really a fine violinist, one of the
 best. A great man.

Pat:  Even greater than Lurch?

5 Arnold:  Well . . . in his way. Tosca is a celebrity after all.

Pat:  He must be. To have a dinner in his honor at the Orion. Which way do we go, Arnold?

Arnold:  Right up these steps and then left, I think. The ballroom.

Pat:  Wow, look at this place. It's a palace.

Arnold:  Nobody's even here yet. Let's wait outside, OK? I'm too nervous to go in. Besides,

10  we can't be the first ones there.

Pat:  Sit down out here, Arnold, and let me look at you in your suit and tie. You ought to
 dress up more often.

Arnold:  Cement-mixers don't often mix in this kind of society.

Pat:  You got tickets to Rhoda Tosca's dinner, didn't you?

15 Arnold:  *Rotl.* And I only got tickets because Mr. Tosca and my father once studied together.

Pat:  No kidding! Arnold, you're practically a celebrity yourself!

Arnold:  Not quite. And not for long. I can't even stay at the ball until midnight. I've got
 to turn into a pumpkin, get back home and work on my project.

Pat:  How can you work on it at home?

20 Arnold:  I took all the source materials on my topic home with me.

Pat:  Arnold, you're not supposed to take those things out of the library. Why did you do
 that?

Arnold:  Well, it's convenient after all.

Pat:  Wait a minute. Isn't Dick Crosby working on the same topic as you?

25 Arnold:  Could be. I really don't know.

Pat:  You *know* he is!

Arnold:  Well, that's just his tough luck.

Pat:  Arnold, you're deliberately trying to ruin his chances!

Arnold:  Oh, my God! That's him, Tosca, coming up the steps. Pat, let's talk about this

30  later, OK?

Pat:  Let's talk about it *now*, Arnold!

Arnold:  Look, sweet, will you, please? He's coming over here.

Pat:  Don't you try to change the subject. That was really a dirty trick, Arnold, taking out
 all those books.

35 Arnold:  Pat, please don't cause me any trouble now. Smile, damn it!

Mr. Tosca:  Good evening. Going to dinner?

Arnold:  Yes, sir. We were just going in.

Pat:  You can just go in by yourself, you little rat!

Arnold:  Pat, will you shut up!

40 Pat:  I won't take that kind of talk from you, Arnold!

Mr. Tosca: Arnold? Well, so it is. I hardly recognized you after all these years.

Pat: You meatball!

Mr. Tosca: How's your mother?

Arnold: She's fine, sir. She sends her best.

45 Mr. Tosca: Arnold, let's try to get together and talk a little later, all right? A pleasure to meet you, Miss . . . . .

Pat: Bevierre.

Mr. Tosca: Miss Bevierre. I hope you two will manage to settle your differences in the meantime.

50 Arnold: Pat, how could you embarrass me like that?

Pat: So you're going to put the blame on me, are you? Well *I* won't be embarrassing *you* any more *this* evening, Arnold Bixby. You and Rotl Whozit can have a pleasant little chat together, just the two of you. Good night!

Questions:

1. What does Arnold mean when he says they "can't be the first ones there"?
2. What (or who) is Arnold referring to when he talks of staying "at the ball until midnight" and turning "into a pumpkin"?
3. What words and expressions does Arnold use that make Pat especially angry?

**I   Production**

---

*Generalization:*  Yes / No question intonation usually rises at the last stressed syllable at the end of the sentence. But if the speaker places special emphasis on a word earlier in the sentence, the intonation rises at that point of emphasis. (See Lesson 21 for Special Emphasis and Falling Intonation) Example:

Did Dick buy Harriet a Spanish dictionary for her bir⌐thday? (Normal Intonation)

a.  Special Emphasis on *Spanish:*
   Did Dick buy Harriet a Sp⌐anish dictionary for her birthday?
b.  Special Emphasis on *Harriet:*
   Did Dick buy ⌐Harriet a Spanish dictionary for her birthday?
c.  Special Emphasis on *Dick:*
   Did ⌐Dick buy Harriet a Spanish dictionary for her birthday?

---

1  —  Repetition  —

1. Are you taking the bus to South Park this we⌐ekend?
2. Are you taking the bus to South Park⌐ this weekend?
3. Are you taking the bus to So⌐uth Park this weekend?
4. Are you taking the b⌐us to South Park this weekend?
5. Are y⌐ou taking the bus to South Park this weekend?

2  —  Practice  —
Listen and repeat the sentence; then say the sentence again applying special emphasis to the cue word.

1. Do you have to type the paper your⌐self?
T    *type*           S1    Do you have to⌐ *type* the paper yourself?
     *have to*         S2    Do you *ha⌐ve to* type the paper yourself?
     *you*
2. Did you telephone your parents last we⌐ekend?
T    *parents*
     *telephone*
     *you*
3. Will Pat sell her car before the end of the⌐ term?
     *before*
     *car*
     *Pat*
4. Wouldn't he like to have lunch with us next Sa⌐turday?
     *next*
     *us*
     *lunch*
     *like*

this exercise continued on next page

5. Can we finish our project before the fifteenth of the m/onth?
>    *fifteenth*
>    *our*
>    *we*
>    *can*

## II  Identification and Practice

1  —  Practice  —

Listen and repeat the sentence; then apply special emphasis to the cue word. When you answer the questions *deny* the point that is emphasized.

1. Are you going to wash your car Sunday mo/rning?

| T | *Sunday* | S1 | Are you going to wash your car *Su/nday* morning? |
|---|---|---|---|
|   |          | S2 | No. (I'm going to wash it tomorrow.) |
|   | *car*    | S2 | Are you going to wash your /car Sunday morning? |
|   |          | S3 | No. (I'm going to wash my clothes.) |
|   | *your*   | S3 | Are you going to wash /*your* car Sunday morning? |
|   |          | S4 | No. (I'm going to wash Alice's car.) |
|   | *you*    |    |    |

2. Should I leave a big tip for the head /waiter?

T    *big*
     *I*

3. Didn't your brother take two courses in biology last/ term?

T    *biology*
     *two*
     *your*

4. Did you watch the six o'clock news last /night?

T    *last*
     *six*
     *you*

5. Did you make an appointment for three o'clock next Saturday af/ternoon?

T    *next*
     *three*
     *you*

---

*Note:* Speakers may place special emphasis on two (or more) items in a Yes / No question.
In this case intonation rises on each item that receives special emphasis.
Examples:

You keep a *wa/rthog* in your *be/droom?*
Arnold puts *peanut /butter* on his *c/elery?*

---

2  —  Practice: Double Emphasis  —

1. Arnold puts *peanut| butter* on his *wa/rthog?*
2. You mean you have *al/ligators* in your *bath/tub?*

this exercise continued on next page

3. He talks *Eng/lish* in his *sle/ep?*
4. You keep *sand/wiches* in your *text/book?*


3 — Practice: Double Emphasis —
Examples:

| T | onions / apple pie | S1 | You eat *on/ions* with *app/le pie?* |
|---|---|---|---|
| | | S2 | No. (I eat ice cream with apple pie.) |
| | acid / swimming pool | S2 | You put *ac/id* in your *swi/mming pool?* |
| | | S3 | No. (I put chlorine in my swimming pool.) |

ink / hair
grass / salad
tea / gas tank
homework / vacation
gasoline / sink
salad dressing / soup
ice cream / oven
shoe polish / toothbrush


4 — Practice: Polite Suggestions —
Situation: "Ending the Party"
You have a party at your apartment Friday evening. At 2:00 a.m. everyone has left except your friend Carlos who has drunk too much and does not seem to want to leave. Select one student to be Carlos. *Using questions,* the others suggest to Carlos that the party is over and it is time to go home.

Example questions:

| S1 | Do you want me to call a taxi for you, Carlos? | Carlos: No, I can drive home. |
|---|---|---|
| S2 | Don't you have a class early tomorrow morning? | No, tomorrow is a holiday. |
| S3 | Would you like a cup of coffee before you go? | No, maybe later, thanks. |
| | Don't you have to work tomorrow? | |
| | Have you got transportation home? | |
| | Is there anything on TV this late at night? | |
| | Would you rather spend the night on the couch? | |


3 — Dialog —
Listen to the following dialog and answer the questions at the end.


After the Party


Harriet: You drink your coffee black, Bob?
Robert: What? Coffee? No, cream and sugar please . . . Wait a minute. I don't want any coffee.
Richard: I'm afraid that's all we've got left. Coffee and a few cans of milk for the dog.
5      And a piece of birthday cake.

Robert:  You should a saved a couple beers for the dog. It's his birthday after all.

Richard:  No, it's *my* birthday. The dog was just a present, remember?

Harriet:  Here's your coffee.

Robert:  Thanks, Harriet. Hey, whatdya takin' that away for? I haven't finished it.

10    Harriet:  It's already warm, Bob.

Richard:  You don't want any warm beer, do you?

Robert:  I don't care if it's warm.

Harriet:  Bob, don't you think I should call you a cab? I'm going to call you a cab now, all right?

15    Robert:  Whatdya say we all go out for a little breakfast?

Richard:  I just want to go to bed.

Harriet:  Dick!

Robert:  A party-pooper, eh? You must be getting old.

Richard:  Well, I do need my four hours of sleep a night. Don't you have to get up

20       tomorrow and work on your project for Lurch?

Robert:  No, I'm almost done. I'm just going to relax tomorrow. Watch the game on TV.

Harriet:  There, you see, Dick? I told you you should have started earlier. Now you'll be lucky to finish in time.

Richard:  I may not get it done at all if Pat was telling the truth about Arnold.

25    Robert:  Nice little birthday treachery, Dick. Arnold has always had it in for you.

Richard:  Well, why should he? I've never done him any harm.

Harriet:  Maybe Pat was mistaken about this. She seemed awfully upset this evening.

Robert:  Arnold is a rotten fink. Pat's right about that.

Harriet:  Here comes your taxi, Bob.

30    Robert:  Well, I guess I better say good night. Thanks for the party and all the hospitality.

Harriet:  Thank *you* for keeping "dog" for us.

Robert:  That's OK. We got along fine. Dick, I'm sorry I drank up all your beer.

Richard:  That's all right. That's what it's for.

35    Robert:  Bye now. See you next week.

Richard:  Good night, Bob.

Harriet:  You know, after the first shock, Bob really got along fine with "dog."

Richard:  Good old "dog." We'd better give him a name, don't you think? How about "Arnold"?

40    Harriet:  Don't be so rash. Telephone Arnold in the morning and ask him about the books. I can't believe he'd really try to ruin your chances to pass the course.

Richard:  Pat seemed to think so.

Harriet:  Well, she and Arnold don't get along very well, that's all.

Richard:  OK, babe, I'll call him tomorrow. Some real work has got to be done this weekend.

45       One way or another that paper has to get itself written.


Questions:

1. Why do they want to give Bob coffee to drink?
2. Harriet calls out "Dick!" as though she disapproved of something he said. What?
3. Does Bob speak in a "different" way? How is his speech different from that of the others? Why?

# LESSON TWENTY-FOUR /l/ and /r/ clusters —

## I  Recognition and Production

### 1  — Repetition —

| | | |
|---|---|---|
| blend | called | health |
| blast | filled | shelf |
| class | built | film |
| clean | silk | golf |
| climb | milk | bulb |

| | | | |
|---|---|---|---|
| bridge | greed | art | horse |
| brand | breeze | arthritis | first |
| practice | throw | birth | thirsty |
| trust | scratch | born | worst |
| thrill | scream | learn | world |

## II  Stress

### 1  — Repetition —

a bláde of gráss  
a drúnken párty  
a cálled stríke  

a gréat pléasure  
crówded stréets  
a thrílling mélodrama  

Scréam for hélp.  
Drínk your mílk.  
She was thrówn by a hórse.  
They áll súffered from arthrítis.  

### 2  — Read and Look Up.

1. The hardest thing was driving through the crowded streets.
2. Learning to drive was hardly worth the effort.
3. He crashed into the bridge on his way home from the party.
4. They called it the worst of all possible worlds.
5. We had a very pleasant flight to San Francisco.
6. She called the waiters over to the table to observe the fly at the bottom of the glass.
7. The workers called a wildcat strike for Thursday and Friday.
8. She drank three quarts of ale this morning for breakfast.
9. Place the bottle of milk on the shelf next to the bread.
10. The broken glass scratched his arm when it struck him.

90

**III Intonation — Series / Surprise**

*Generalization:* Items in a series often take rising intonation. The last item in a series making up an ordinary sentence will, however, take a falling intonation.

   Examples:

   I'd like a hambu/rger, a c/oke, an order of/fries, a chocolate mi/lkshake, and a piece of ca\ke.

   We washed/the car, waxed/it, cleaned out the/closets, cut the/grass, burned the/trash, and went to a mov\ie.

1 — Repetition —

1. We had a flat/tire, ran out of/gas, lost our trav/eller's checks, and then got lo\st.
2. The price was $4.00 for the ti/ckets, $10.00 for din/ner, $5.00 for the/movie, and $20.00 for the ho\tel.
3. In our class we had two Li/byans, five Venez/uelans, four/Thais, a Ja/panese, and two Mexi\cans.
4. I'm going to take a/nap, have di/nner, watch/TV, and then go st\udy.

2 — Read and Look Up —

1. On the trip I visited Turkey, Greece, Lebanon, and Italy.
2. He ate two bowls of soup, a chicken, four potatoes, and a salad.
3. Before I began classes I saw my advisor, registered, paid tuition, bought books, and found an apartment.
4. When you apply you have to get three references, send all your transcripts, take the TOEFL exam, and hope for the best.

*Generalization:* Question words (*who, what,* etc.) are sometimes spoken with rising intonation. In this case the speaker is not really asking for new information. Rather he wants a repetition or explanation of something which is surprising or hard to believe.

   Examples:

   I'm leaving for home today.                Wh/at?

   He spent his vacation in Antarctica.        Wh/ere?

3 — Repetition —

1. I've just decided to quit school.           W/hat?
   Yes. I'm tired of studying.

2. I just talked to the President the other day.    W/ho?
   The President of the Student Council.

this exercise continued on next page

3. We're having breakfast tomorrow at six a.m.                    Wh⌐en?
   At six. I have to be at work early.


4 — Practice: Surprise Intonation —
Examples:

|  |  |  |  |
|---|---|---|---|
| T | where / study next year (Guam) | S1 | Where are you going to study next year? |
|  |  | S2 | In Guam. |
|  |  | S1 | Wh⌐ere? |
|  |  | S2 | Guam. (It's a nice island in the Pacific.) |
|  | who / talk to before class (the President) | S2 | Who were you talking to before class? |
|  |  | S3 | I was talking to the President. |
|  |  | S2 | W⌐ho? |
|  |  | S3 | The President. (He's a good friend of mine.) |

when / go to the movies (midnight)
what / score on the test (zero)
where / going for lunch (city jail)
how / travelling to Los Angeles (on foot)
who / staying at your house (the mayor)
when / leaving for your country (this afternoon)
where / get a haircut (my aunt's house)
how / lose so much weight (by eating ice cream)


5 — Dialog —
Listen to the following dialog and answer the questions at the end.


### Dick Seeks a New Home

Robert: OK, OK, OK, OK, OK, I'm coming. You don't have to pound the door
　　down . . . Who is it?
Richard: It's me. Open the door, will you please?
Robert: OK. Now who are you?
5　Richard: Open your eyes, Bob. That might help.
Robert: I don't have to. I can tell by the sound of your voice. It's Dick, isn't it?
Richard: Uh-huh.
Robert: Why are you getting me out of bed at this time of night?
Richard: It's eleven-thirty.
10　Robert: In the daytime?
Richard: Yes. You don't look too good. Why don't you sit down and I'll pour some
　　coffee into you.
Robert: How did I get home last night?
Richard: By taxi.
15　Robert: How?
Richard: Taxi. Harriet called a taxi for you.
Robert: I don't remember any taxi.
Richard: Here, drink this. Maybe your memory will come back. I need your brain for a
20　　few minutes.
Robert: Ask me for anything else, Dick.

Richard: No brain there, huh?

Robert: I'm sorry.

Richard: I have a little problem and I need your help.

25 Robert: You want me to keep "dog" back here for a while?

Richard: No, I want you to keep *me* here.

Robert: What? Did Harriet throw you out?

Richard: Not exactly, but I'm afraid we got some bad news this morning.

Robert: What?

30 Richard: Well, first I called Arnold to get those books I need. He said he didn't know what I was talking about.

Robert: He's a rotten fink, Dick.

Richard: And then Harriet got a phone call from her mother. She's coming to visit next week and so I need a place to stay.

35 Robert: What?

Richard: Harriet's mother's coming.

Robert: Here?

Richard: Are you awake?

Robert: What?

40 Richard: Wake up, will you? I'm asking if I can move in with you for a few days.

Robert: You mean Harriet's mother doesn't like you?

Richard: Worse than that.

Robert: She hates you.

Richard: Worse than that.

45 Robert: What's worse than that?

Richard: She doesn't know that we're married. Harriet's parents never approved of me.

Robert: And so you haven't told them yet. Dick, I'd like to help you out, but uh . . .

Richard: You can't?

Robert: Look, my brother and his wife are coming Monday afternoon. They could be

50 staying here for weeks. I just don't have enough room, that's all.

Richard: Well, thanks anyway. If worst comes to worst I can try a hotel—or sleep in the school bus.

Robert: Not that! Why don't you just surprise your in-laws?

Richard: No thanks. I don't need any more surprises. Just a little peace and quiet.

Questions:

1. Why would Robert not remember how he got home the night before?
2. *Underline* the question words in the dialog that have rising intonation.
3. When Dick says "You can't?", he seems to *know* that Robert won't be able to help him. How does he know?
4. Is Robert annoyed when he hears someone knocking on his door? How can you tell?
5. Would young people in your country marry in secret? What would be the reaction?

# LESSON TWENTY-FIVE — Affixes and Stress Shift

## I Suffixes with NO Stress Change

> *Generalization:* When added to a word, some suffixes do not cause a change in stress. These suffixes include *-ness, -ship, -ance, -able, -ful, -al, -hood, -ment, -er/or, -ly,* and *-ist.* Ask your teacher the part of speech that results from adding the suffix.

### 1 — Repetition —

| | | | |
|---|---|---|---|
| háppy | háppi*ness* | devélop | devélop*ment* |
| thórough | thórough*ness* | encóurage | encóurage*ment* |
| adúlt | adúl*thood* | méasure | méasure*ment* |
| néighbor | néighbor*hood* | repláce | repláce*ment* |
| cráftsman | cráftsman*ship* | atténd | atténd*ance* |
| friénd | friénd*ship* | insúre | insúr*ance* |
| óperate | ópera*tor* | propóse | propós*al* |
| démonstrate | démonstra*tor* | appróve | appróv*al* |
| týpe | týp*ist* | fárm | fárm*er* |
| biólogy | biólog*ist* | wórk | wórk*er* |

| | |
|---|---|
| rápid | rápid*ly* |
| prófit | prófit*able* |
| wónder | wónder*ful* |
| béauty | béauti*ful* |

### 2 — Practice: Suffixes / No Stress Change —

When you hear the teacher say a word from Section 1 above, respond with the corresponding word of the pair.

Examples:

| T | | S | |
|---|---|---|---|
| | háppy | | háppiness |
| | fárm | | fármer |
| | adúlthood | | adúlt |
| | biólogy | | biólogist |
| | insúrance | | insúre |
| | rápid | | _____ |
| | propósal | | _____ |
| | etc. | | |

## II   Suffixes with Stress Change

> *Generalization:* When suffixes like *-ity, -ar/al, -cal,* and *-tion* are added to words, stress may move toward the end of the words. Note the change from one part of speech to another when the suffix is added.

1   —   Repetition   —

| Adjectives | Nouns | Verbs | Nouns |
|---|---|---|---|
| stúpid | stupídity | génerate | generátion |
| respónsible | responsibílity | líberate | liberátion |
| áctive | actívity | imágine | imaginátion |
| cápable | capabílity | démonstrate | demonstrátion |
| sénsitive | sensitívity | éducate | educátion |
| sénsible | sensibílity | óperate | operátion |
| rélative | relatívity | órganize | organizátion |

| Nouns | Adjectives |
|---|---|
| hístory | histórical |
| biólogy | biológical |
| geólogy | geológical |
| áccident | accidéntal |
| expériment | experiméntal |
| fámily | famíliar |

2   —   Practice: Suffixes with Stress Change   —
When you hear the teacher say a word from 1 above, respond with the contrasting form.
   Examples:

| T | | S | |
|---|---|---|---|
| stúpid | | stupídity | |
| génerate | | generátion | |
| operátion | | óperate | |
| geológical | | geólogy | |
| fámily | | | |
| sensibílity | | | |
| etc. | | | |

**III   Stress**

1  —  Repetition  —

| | |
|---|---|
| devéloping cóuntries | a péaceful demonstrátion |
| the biológical sciénces | a thórough investigátion |
| a quíet neighborhood | an éducated minórity |
| a dífficult operátion | a sýstem of méasurement |

Úse your imaginátion.
She's véry áctive in the histórical society.
We encóurage rápid devélopment.
The néighbors are véry hélpful.

2  —  Identification  —
Listen to the following sentences and mark the stressed syllables.
  Example:

They órganize stúdent actívities.

1. Economic development in neighboring countries has slowed down.
2. They were active in the neighborhood educational organization.
3. My parents encouraged me to complete my education.
4. A demonstration is being organized for tomorrow.
5. He's insured against all kinds of accidents.

3  —  Read and Look Up  —

1. He investigated his own family history.
2. The old system of measurement will gradually be replaced.
3. Because her family didn't approve, she gave up geological research.
4. The demonstrators denied responsibility for the accident.
5. We accidentally forgot to renew the insurance policy.
6. I always imagined that operations would be covered by the insurance.
7. Sensible people prefer comfort and profit to liberation.

4  —  Practice: Suffixes  —
Answer the following questions using a different form of the underlined word.
  Examples:

| | | | |
|---|---|---|---|
| T | Did you have your *operation* yet? | S1 | No, the doctor doesn't want to *operate* until next month. |
| T | Are you *responsible* for the money? | S2 | No, I don't have any *responsibilities*. |
| T | Did you ever *imagine* you might be rich someday? | S3 | No, I have no *imagination*. (Yes, but only in my *imagination*.) |

Is there any *profit* in working for the government?
Are you *active* in any social organization?
Would you like to *demonstrate* against (the President)?

this exercise continued on next page

Do you live in a good *neighborhood*?

Can you tell us about the *historical* development of your country?

Is the system of *measurement* in your country different from here?

Is the economy in (Bolivia) *developing* rapidly?

Did your parents give you much *encouragement* to get an education?

Do you *insure* your luggage when you travel?

Are you interested in studying *biology*?


5 — Dialog —

Listen to the following dialog and answer the questions at the end.


### Harriet's Parents Come to Visit

Mrs. Belenson:  Harriet, where in the world did all these beer bottles come from?

Harriet:  I had a little party here, Mom. A birthday party with lots of guests.

Mrs. Belenson:  It must have been quite a celebration. Your friends certainly drink
a lot, don't they? Whose birthday was it?

5   Harriet:  Oh, just a friend's.

Mr. Belenson:  You might send us a little news once in a while. We always imagine the
worst when we don't hear from you.

Harriet:  Don't let your imagination run away with you, Daddy. I'm really doing fine
here. I've just been busy, that's all.

10   Mr. Belenson:  Are you taking courses this semester? You've got a lot of academic-type
books around.

Harriet:  Uh, nope. But I might take something next term.

Mrs. Belenson:  Good for you, Harriet. You get as much education as you can.

Harriet:  Daddy, will you help me with these bottles? I want to throw the whole mess

15   out.

Mrs. Belenson:  Harriet! What in the world! Have you ever seen so many cigar butts?

Harriet:  Oops, I forgot about those.

Mr. Belenson:  Not yours, I hope.

Harriet:  No, Daddy, from the party.

20   Mrs. Belenson:  For Goodness' Sake, take these smelly things out too.

Harriet:  OK, Mom. Oh darn, now what? Will you take this stuff for me while I get
the phone.

Mrs. Belenson:  I'll get it, dear . . . Hello? Yes, she is. Who is it please? Oh . . . I see.
Just a moment. Harriet, it's for you. It's that Dick Crawley fellow.

25   Harriet:  I'll take it, Mom.

Mrs. Belenson:  You're not still seeing *him*, are you?

Harriet:  Well, I see him once in a while. He's not a monster, you know.

Mrs. Belenson:  Harriet! How could you? You know how your father and I feel about
that . . . that . . . good-for-nothing. I'm just going to tell him that you're not in.

30   Harriet:  Mother, may I have the telephone please . . .

Mrs. Belenson:  Harriet, you're making a big mistake, giving a boy like that false hopes.

Harriet:  I'll take care of him, Mom.

Mr. Belenson:  Gretchen, calm down. You shouldn't go on and on about this Crosgood
fellow. Harriet's not the kind of girl to be bossed around by us any more. It's a new

35   generation, Gretch.

Mrs. Belenson:  I don't boss people around, Arthur.

Mr. Belenson:  Only because they won't stand for it. Don't you see you're just
    encouraging her to see this fellow? Think for a minute of what we might get
    stuck with for a son-in-law.
40  Mrs. Belenson:  Please, don't even say it. It's too horrid.
Mr. Belenson:  OK, I won't say it. But it could happen. Use a little psychology, and
    Harriet will see this guy for what he really is. Whatever that might be.
Mrs. Belenson:  A nobody!
Harriet:  Mother, are you two talking about my boy friends again?
45  Mrs. Belenson:  No, dear, I was just thinking out loud that nobody as intelligent as
    you should . . .
Mr. Belenson:  Gretchen!
Mrs. Belenson:  . . . should have to cook. How about letting your father and me treat
    you to dinner out this evening?
50  Harriet:  It's a deal!


Questions:

1. At the end when Mr. Belenson interrupts his wife, what does he think she is about to say?
2. Does Mr. Belenson like Richard? How would he handle the situation?

# LESSON TWENTY-SIX — Clusters with /s/ —

## I    Recognition and Production

### 1   — Repetition —

| | | | | | |
|---|---|---|---|---|---|
| sleep | Spain | stick | small | strike | spring |
| slight | speed | stay | smoke | stress | spread |
| slip | speak | square | snack | string | scratch |
| slow | spend | squeak | sweep | straw | scream |
| slap | spoon | squall | swat | strange | scrape |

| | | | | |
|---|---|---|---|---|
| laughs | rats | lacks | priced | lists |
| chiefs | cheats | drinks | east | costs |
| lamps | hunts | links | cost | tastes |
| hips | prince | strikes | taste | tasks |

## II   Stress

### 1   — Repetition —

the lówest príce

slý óld fóx

slíghtly scréwy

sléepless níghts

a squéaky spríng

eást and wést

míxed drínks

pérma-press slácks

Fáce the fácts.

He's sómewhat scáred of cáts.

It's the bést you've éver tásted.

She spéaks Spánish with a stróng áccent.

### 2   — Read and Look Up —

1. He reduced his speed when he saw a police car.
2. Would you speak more slowly, please?
3. Milkshakes are priced so high I've forgotten what they taste like.
4. We spent many sleepless nights studying for the tests.
5. Lists of students enrolled in the course are posted in the office.
6. Despite low test scores she got into graduate school.
7. Every student in the seminar class is too scared to speak.
8. We spent all last spring in Spain going to school.

**III   Intonation**

1 — Review of Patterns: Repetition —

Questions                                          Answers

1. He laughs at all your jo\kes, doesn't /he?      Yes, but I still don't like\ him.
2. What's that squeaking sound in the eng\ine?     It's not the engine, it's the bra\kes.
3. She cheats on te\sts, doesn't \she?             No, she lacks the skill to cheat success\fully.
4. He keeps old bits of string and steals from     Yes, he's slightly scre\wy, you know.
   the servants—isn't that /strange?
5. If the host falls asleep, it's time to say      When the host stops mixing drinks, it's time
   goodnight, don't you think?                      to lea\ve.


2 — Practice: Question and Answer Chain (/s/ clusters) —
   Example:

   S1   ask   S2   how many hours he sleeps at night.
               S1   How many hours do you sleep each night?
               S2   (I sleep a lot on weekends, but not much before tests.)
   S2   ask   S3   how much it costs to buy a pair of skis.
                    if there are many strikes in this country.
                    which he likes best—milkshakes, banana splits, or ice cream sundaes.
                    if he can mix drinks.
                    if he has stopped smoking.
                    if he is scared of snakes.
                    if he studied for a test last night.
                    how many speeches he has made.
                    if he spends much money on high-priced clothing.
                    if he has ever invested money in the stock market.
                    if he speaks (   ) slowly.


3 — Dialog —
Listen to the following dialog and answer the questions at the end.


At the Hotel

   Richard:  It's about time you showed up!
   Harriet:  Well, I couldn't just walk out from under my parents' noses, could I? Here,
      I brought you something.
   Richard:  Sandwiches! Good girl! Did you bring any money too?
5  Harriet:  No cash. But I got your checkbook. Good Lord, you should have seen me.
      I hid all your things under the bed and I was sniffing around with "Dog" looking
      for your checkbook. "Dog" found it; you can see where he chewed it up a little.
   Richard:  Good old "Dog." Already he likes the taste of money.
   Harriet:  But here, Dick. Here is the best gift of all.
10 Richard:  What is it?
   Harriet:  Remember the books and articles you said you needed for your paper?

Richard:  Yeah?

Harriet:  Well, there they are.

Richard:  I can't believe it. How did you get this stuff?

15   Harriet:  *I* didn't get it. *Pat* brought it all over to the apartment.

Richard:  Pat! How did *she* get it? Arnold wouldn't give it up without a fight.

Harriet:  He probably doesn't even know yet. Pat said she just walked over to Arnold's house and asked his mother for the books.

Richard:  Good old Pat. But nasty old Arnold. Bob is right about him.

20   Harriet:  Rotten fink?

Richard:  Uh-huh. Look at all this stuff. Arnold's going to explode when he finds out. I wish I could see that.

Harriet:  Just get to work. How much time do you have left?

Richard:  A couple of days. And nights. I'd better work straight through.

25   Harriet:  I'll stop back, OK, Dick? I've got to run now. My parents must be getting nervous.

Richard:  Who's nervous? You're the one who looks scared to death. You think they followed you here?

Harriet:  Please, don't even say it.

30   Richard:  They could be standing outside the door right now, ready to break it down and rescue you.

Harriet:  I can imagine what they'd do to you.

Richard:  They don't like me too much, do they?

Harriet:  Well, Mother doesn't think your "prospects" are too good.

35   Richard:  Where could she get an idea like that?

Harriet:  I can't imagine. But, then, Mother doesn't even like "Dog."

Richard:  What?

Harriet:  "Dog" bit Daddy on the leg. Mother said I should have him put away.

Richard:  Poor "Daddy."

40   Harriet:  No, put "Dog" away, you idiot. I told her I couldn't because he was a gift from a friend.

Richard:  And she wanted to know who your friend was, right?

Harriet:  Right. I'm afraid she's getting awfully suspicious about my "friends."


Questions:

1. When Dick says "Yeah?" why is it a question?
2. Who is the "rotten fink" that Harriet refers to?
3. What does Dick mean when he says he'll have to work "straight through"?
4. What are "prospects"? Are Dick's "prospects" good?

# LESSON TWENTY-SEVEN — Affixation and Vowel Change —

## I  Recognition and Production

> *Generalization:* Vowel changes associated with affixation.

### 1 — Repetition —

| /ey/ | /æ/ | /(y)uw/ | /ə/ |
|------|-----|---------|-----|
| vain | vanity | assume | assumption |
| nation | national | resume | resumption |
| nature | natural | reduce | reduction |
| depraved | depravity | presume | presumption |
| sane | sanity | produce | production |
| grateful | gratitude | consume | consumption |

### 2 — Practice —

When you hear the teacher say one form of a word from the above lists, respond with the other form of the same word.

Examples:

| T | vain | S | vanity |
|---|------|---|--------|
| T | natural | S | nature |

### 3 — Repetition —

| /iy/ | /e/ | /ow/ | /a/ |
|------|-----|------|-----|
| brief | brevity | compose | composite |
| deep | depth | phone | phonic |
| reveal | revelation | pose | posture |
| preside | president | impose | imposter |
| precede | precedent | evoke | evocative |
| appeal | appellative | provoke | provocative |
| obscene | obscenity | | |

### 4 — Practice —

When you hear the teacher say one form of a word from the above lists, respond with the other form of the same word.

Examples:

| T | brevity | S | brief |
|---|---------|---|-------|
| T | compose | S | composite |

5  —  Repetition  —

|     /ay/     |     /i/     |
|-------------|-------------|
| wide | width |
| wise | wisdom |
| divide | division |
| hostile | hostility |
| reconcile | reconciliation |
| inspire | inspiration |
| realize | realization |
| conspire | conspiracy |

6  —  Practice  —

When you hear the teacher say one form of a word from the above lists, respond with the other form of the same word.

Examples:

| T | wide | S | width |
|---|------|---|-------|
| T | conspiracy | S | conspire |

II   Stress

1  —  Repetition  —

without précedent                          extrémely gráteful
the nátional débt                          the presíding júdge
Repúblican nátional convéntion             a scientífic expedítion
a revísed edítion                          unreconciled conflicts

Divíde and cónquer.
Brévity is the sóul of wít.
My sýmpathies gó with the Présidént.

2  —  Read and Look Up  —

1. Vanity is only natural, isn't it?
2. Insanity is no excuse for profanity.
3. An apology should precede reconciliation.
4. Reconciliation holds no appeal for someone as ungrateful as Arnold.
5. In a moment of inspiration she realized how the accident must have occurred.
6. Dick composed an extremely obscene poem and attached it to a get-well card.
7. Arnold may make an appeal for sympathy by posing as an invalid.
8. Harriet suggested sending Arnold on an expedition to the North Pole.
9. He appealed to the Dean for permission to drop out of school for reasons of health.
10. Deprived of the opportunity for employment he may have to abandon his academic career.

## III Intonation

### 1 — Review: Repetition —

| Questions | Answers |
|---|---|

1. You don't object to profanity in spe|ech, do/you?

It's all right if you're profane in modera\tion.

2. Why don't you two reconcile your dif\ferences?

I think an apology should precede reconcilia\tion.

3. Did you expect him to show much gratitude for your gen/erosity?

I thought he might be at least a little\grateful.

4. Would you accept leadership in an expedition to the North/Pole?

Do you think I'm in/sane?

### 2 — Practice —

Restate the following sentences, using your own words. Use another form for each underlined word. Use as many (or as few) words as you need.

Examples:

Arnold always assumed that *conspiracies* were everywhere.

S: Arnold thought that people were always conspiring against him.

The depth of his *wisdom* was not great.

S: He was not really very wise.

1. *Gratitude* and *generosity* were foreign to Arnold's character.
2. *Reconciliation* was less appealing to Arnold than continued *hostility*.
3. Harriet's *suggestion* that Arnold be sent to the North Pole was not taken seriously.
4. An act of *hostility* rarely evokes sympathy.
5. The *assumption* that Arnold was seriously injured was false.
6. The *resumption* of hostilities was foreseen by all.
7. Appeals for assistance often evoke responses of great *generosity*.
8. The *realization* that he would be deprived of employment only raised Arnold's natural level of irritation.
9. He felt there was a *conspiracy* to deprive him of his job.
10. By posing as a helpless invalid Arnold led many to doubt his *sanity*.

### 3 — Dialog —

Listen to the following dialog and answer the questions at the end.

#### After the Accident

Pat: Oh, Bob, am I glad to see you! Where is he?

Bob: Upstairs. Come on, I'll show you the way.

Pat: What happened anyway? His mother sounded awfully upset on the phone. Is she still here?

5 Bob: Just left.

Pat: Well? How is he?

Bob: OK, I guess, under the circumstances. You'll see for yourself. I should warn you, though, that he's not in a very good mood.

Pat: What do you mean?

10  Bob: He's blaming the accident on all his friends, including you.

Pat: Well, I'm afraid I may be partly responsible. I did something that upset him.

Bob: OK. I just wanted to give you a chance to prepare yourself. He's healthy enough
to be nasty.

Pat: Oh, let's go in. I'm as composed as I can get.

15  Arnold: Hah! I wondered when *you* would show up! Now all we need is Crosby himself
to come in with a bouquet of flowers.

Pat: I brought you a few things, Arnold.

Arnold: Oh? Textbooks perhaps?

Pat: Arnold, I do want to apologize. If what I did or said had anything to do with your

20  accident, I'm sorry.

Arnold: It was no accident!

Pat: What are you saying?

Bob: He thinks Gus and the others at the construction site did this on purpose.

Pat: Did what? Arnold, what happened to you anyway?

25  Bob: His vanity was shattered.

Arnold: The doctors aren't sure yet. I may be suffering from severe internal injuries.

Bob: Entirely cranial, I suspect.

Arnold: I resent your bedside manner, you quack!

Pat: Arnold, are you in some kind of cast?

30  Bob: That's part of the story. You see, Arnold was driving the cement truck.

Pat: I don't see what that's got to do with anything.

Arnold: It's not *my* job to drive the truck. I don't see how they can blame *me* for
what happened.

Bob: They dared him to drive it.

35  Pat: Who?

Bob: Gus and the other men. But Arnold backed it into a pile of bricks, and then he got
out to take a look.

Arnold: I was assessing damages. Not *one* brick broken!

Bob: Then, uh . . . I forget. What happened next, Arnold?

40  Arnold: I don't recall. I think the truck rolled over me.

Bob: No, no, I remember. The truck started to roll backwards and it bumped Arnold
into the cellar.

Pat: The truck didn't roll in too, did it?

Bob: No. It stopped against the foundation wall. But the impact must have started the

45  cement flowing.

Pat: Oh, no, I think I'm beginning to get the picture. The cement poured into the cellar?

Bob: All over our friend here.

Pat: Good Grief! I can't believe it.

Arnold: If you must laugh, Pat, I wish you would go somewhere else.

50  Bob: And Arnold was covered up to his neck in cement. Gus told me that he and the
others were laughing so hard that by the time they got Arnold out he was stiff as a
board. They had to haul him to the hospital in a truck.

Pat: Oh, Arnold, it's lucky for you they didn't throw you in the river.

Arnold: Very funny. Now, if you don't mind, I think visiting hours are over, and I'd like

55  to ge a little rest.

**this exercise continued on next page**

Questions:

1. What was Arnold's "cast"?
2. Why did Pat apologize? Would *you* apologize under the same circumstances? Explain.
3. At the very end (last sentence) what is Arnold trying to get his visitors to do? Is he being polite?

## LESSON TWENTY-EIGHT — Suffixes and Stress Change; Falling Intonation in Yes / No Questions

**I  Recognition and Production**

> *Generalization:* When some ednings, such as -ic, -(i)cal, -(a)tion, and -ial are added to to words, stress shifts toward the end of the word. The vowel of the new stressed syllable may be changed. Note that the part of speech changes when the suffix is added.
>
> Examples:
>
> | | |
> |---|---|
> | sýllable | syllábic |
> | éditor | editórial |
> | exámine | examinátion |

1 — Stress and Vowel Change: Repetition —

| Verb | Noun | Noun | Adjective |
|------|------|------|-----------|
| édit | edítion | pólitics | polítical |
| exámine | examinátion | biógraphy | biográphical |
| órganize | organizátion | philosóphy | philosóphical |
| prepáre | preparátion | éditor | editórial |
| antícipate | anticipátion | science | scientífic |
| expéct | expectátion | réal | realístic |
| partícipate | participátion | sýllable | syllábic |
| consérve | conservátion | geólogy | geológical |

2 — Practice —
When you hear a *verb* form, say the *noun* form. Or, if you hear the *noun* form, say the *verb* form.
  Examples:

  T:  édit                    S:  edítion
      organizátion                órganize

  1. édit
  2. expéct
  3. preparátion
  4. exámine
  5. anticipátion

3 — Practice —
When you hear the *noun* form, say the *adjective* form. If you hear the *adjective* form, say the *noun* form.
  Examples:

  T:  science                 S:  scientífic
      polítical                   pólitics

this exercise continued on next page

1. pólitics
2. éditor
3. philósophy
4. syllábic
5. scíence

## II  Stress

### 1 — Repetition —

revolútionary actívities
polítical opposítion
áctive participátion
an únexpécted announcement

económically únderdevéloped
múlti-syllábic wórds
a crítical editórial
a proféssor of philósophy

We expéct a polítical solútion.
The editórial was véry crítical.
The néw edítion is being prepáred.

### 2 — Read and Look Up —

1. Her timidity kept her from participating.
2. The announcement was completely unexpected.
3. The governor was opposed to student participation in politics.
4. Accurate biographical data was not available.
5. They were vigorous supporters of conservation.
6. He feared participation in philosophical discussions.
7. Most Congressmen can't expect anyone to write biographies of their lives.
8. She entered the university without adequate academic preparation.
9. Never before had the country been more highly developed economically.
10. He accused the conservative party of having no real political philosophy.

## III  Intonation

*Generalization:*  Sometimes falling intonation occurs with Yes / No questions. This may happen if someone asks a series of questions at one time, as in an interview or interrogation. Yes / No questions with falling intonation are ordinarily *not* as polite as those with rising intonation.

1  —  Questions (Falling Intonation) and Answers: Repetition  —

| Questions | Answers |
|---|---|

1. Did you get a college educ\ation?

    Yes, I received my education in (Saudi Ara\bia).

2. Were you active in the political opposition in your coun\try?

    No, I've always been opposed to opposi\tion.

3. Have you ever participated in revolutionary activ\ities?

    No, I've always supported conservatism in gove\rnment.

4. Do you intend to engage in political disturbances in this\ country?

    No, I just want to observe the political institu\tions.

5. Do you promise to be a good\ (boy)?

    Yes, I d\o. (No, I don't.)

2  —  Practice: Interview  —

Select one member of the class to be Arnold, an applicant to the university. Ask Yes / No questions to determine if Arnold is the right sort of person to be allowed to enter a graduate program. Use questions with falling intonation.

    Example questions:

        Do you have ref\erences?
        Were your grades\ good?
        Were you always well-behaved \in school?
        Have you received your B\A?

3  —  Dialog  —

Listen to the following dialog and answer the questions at the end.

Arnold's Telephone Call

Mrs. Belenson: Hello? Hello? Who is it, please?

Arnold: Hello, Harriet?

Mrs. Belenson:  No, it isn't. She's already gone to bed. This is Mrs. Belenson.

Arnold:  Mrs. Who? Harriet, that's you, isn't it? Would you put Richard on the phone,

5      please. I have a few unpleasant words to say to him.

Mrs. Belenson:  I'm sorry, but there's no one here by that name. You must have the wrong number, young man.

Arnold:  Oh . . . I see. I'm awfully sorry. My mistake. Good-bye.

Mrs. Belenson:  Good-bye . . . What a rude fellow! How on earth can Harriet *live* in a town

10     like this? All the people here are utterly mad . . . Oh, no, not again! I hope it's not the same lunatic. Hello?

Arnold:  Harriet! This *is* you, isn't it! I knew it. It's no use trying to disguise your voice.

Mrs. Belenson:  I beg your pardon.

Arnold:  Just tell Richard to come to the phone, please. I want to thank him for putting

15     me in the hospital.

Mrs. Belenson:  Young man, I think that's *exactly* where you belong. And I wish you would stop calling this number.

Arnold:  Harriet, do you deny that this is 536-6744?

Mrs. Belenson:  I do not, but I do deny that I am Harriet. It's obvious that we're not
20      talking about the same person.
Arnold:  I'm talking about Harriet, H-a-r-r-i-e-t. Crosby, C-r-o-s-b-y.
Mrs. Belenson:  Well, there's no one here named . . . Who did you say you wanted to
     talk to?
Arnold:  Harriet. I mean Richard.
25   Mrs. Belenson:  Richard who?
Arnold:  Madame, I am a sick man, calling from my hospital bed. Could you please answer
     a few simple questions?
Mrs. Belenson:  Well, I don't see why . . .
Arnold:  Is Richard there?
30   Mrs. Belenson:  No, there's no one . . .
Arnold:  Will he be home soon?
Mrs. Belenson:  No, I told you . . .
Arnold:  Is Harriet there?
Mrs. Belenson:  Yes, but . . .
35   Arnold:  May I speak to her please?
Mrs. Belenson:  Harriet who?
Arnold:  Harriet Crosby!
Mrs. Belenson:  Who is this speaking, please?
Arnold:  I'm not sure any more.
40   Mrs. Belenson:  Why do you think this Richard fellow would be here?
Arnold:  Well, why not? He lives there, doesn't he?
Mrs. Belenson:  I think you've told me as much as I need to know. Thank you for the
     information.
Arnold:  What information?
45   Mrs. Belenson:  Good-bye.
Arnold:  But . . .
Mrs. Belenson:  Harriet! You come out here this instant!


Questions:

1. Why does Mrs. Belenson say "I beg your pardon"? Is she trying to excuse herself?
2. Mark the Yes / No questions in the dialog in which you *heard* a falling intonation.
3. Can you find any instances of a question word spoken with rising intonation? Why is it
   not the ordinary falling intonation?

# LESSON TWENTY NINE — Affixation and Consonant Change —

## I Recognition and Production

> *Generalization:* The consonant /d/ of some words may change to /ǰ/ when suffixes are added to the word. At the same time vowel change and/or stress shift *may* occur. Note the change in part of speech.
>
> Examples:
>
> | /d/ | /ǰ/ | |
> |---|---|---|
> | résidue | resídual | |
> | gráde | grádual | /ey/-/æ/ |
> | móde | módular | /ow/-/a/ |

### 1 — Repetition —

|  Noun | Adjective | Noun /t/ | Adjective /č/ |
|---|---|---|---|
| (Listen Carefully) | | | |
| múscle | múscular | fáct | fáctual |
| cólumn | cólumnist | right | ríghteous |
| bómb | bombárd | résident | residéntial |
| condémn | condemnátion | président | presidéntial |
| damn | damnátion | /d/ | /ǰ/ |
| sign | signal | résidue | resídual |
| resígn | resignátion | gráde | grádual |
| malígn | malígnant | móde | módular |

### 2 — Practice —

When you hear a word from the above lists, respond with the contrasting form.

Examples:

| T | múscle | S | múscular |
|---|---|---|---|
| | bómb | | bombárd |
| | cólumn | | cólumnist |

| | |
|---|---|
| 1. fact | 6. sign |
| 2. right | 7. malign |
| 3. president | 8. modular |
| 4. grade | 9. damnation |
| 5. resignation | 10. condemn |

*Generalization:* When suffixes are added to some words the consonant /t/ may change to /s/, /d/ to /ž/, or /z/ to /ž/. At the same time vowel change and / or stress shift *may* occur.
Examples:

| /t/ | /s/ |
|-----|-----|
| pírate | píracy |

| /d/ | /ž/ |
|-----|-----|
| explóde | explósion |

| /z/ | /ž/ |
|-----|-----|
| súpervise | supervísion |

3  —  Repetition  —

| Nouns (concrete) /t/ | Nouns (abstract) /s/ | Verbs /d/ | Nouns /ž/ |
|-----|-----|-----|-----|
| pírate | píracy | explóde | explósion |
| président | présidency | províde | provísion |
| lúnatic | lúnacy | divíde | divísion |
| précedent | précedence | | |

| | | /z/ | /ž/ |
|-----|-----|-----|-----|
| | | revise | revision |
| | | supervise | supervision |

| Adjectives | Nouns |
|-----|-----|
| évident | évidence |
| complácent | complácency |

4  —  Practice  —

When you hear a word from the above lists, respond with the contrasting form.
Examples:

| T | pírate | S | píracy |
|---|--------|---|--------|
| T | supervísion | S | súpervise |

| | | | |
|----|----------|-----|-----------|
| 1. | revision | 12. | provision |
| 2. | lunatic | 13. | piracy |
| 3. | evidence | 14. | division |
| 4. | explode | 15 | precedence |
| 5. | complacent | 16. | supervise |
| 6. | residue | 17. | electric |
| 7. | grade | 18. | practical |
| 8. | mode | 19. | physics |
| 9. | divide | 20. | academic |
| 10. | provide | 21. | magic |
| 11. | revise | 22. | music |

> *Generalization:*  When suffixes are added to some words the consonant /k/ may
> change to /s/ or /š/. At the same time vowel change and/or stress shift may
> occur.
>     Examples:
>
> | /k/ | /s/ | /s/ |
> |-----|-----|-----|
> | médical | médicine | medícinal |
>
> | /k/ | /s/ | /š/ |
> |-----|-----|-----|
> | pólitics | pólicy | politícian |

5  —  Repetition  —

| /k/ | /s/ | |
|-----|-----|-----|
| médical | médicine | medícinal |
| crítical | críticism | críticize |
| romántic | románticism | románticize |
| públic | publícity | públicize |

| /k/ | /s/ | /š/ |
|-----|-----|-----|
| pólitics | pólicy | politícian |
| eléctric | electrícity | electrícian |
| práctical | práctice | practícioner |
| phýsics | phýsicist | physícian |
| académic | académicism | academícian |
| mágic | - - - - - - - - | magícian |
| músic | - - - - - - - - | musícian |
| mathemátics | - - - - - - - - | mathematícian |

6  —  Testing  —
When you hear a word from the above lists, respond with *at least* one of the other forms.
    Examples:

| T | pólicy | S | pólitics (or politícian) |
|---|--------|---|--------------------------|
| T | musícian | S | músic |

    1.  electric
    2.  criticize
    3.  practice
    4.  medicinal
    5.  magic
    6.  publicize
    7.  academicism
    8.  romantic
    9.  physics
    10.  politics

## II  Stress

### 1  — Repetition —

a residéntial néighborhood            a médical fáct
fáctual quéstions                     géneral practítioner
the Président's signature             ríghteous indignátion
sénsitive to critícism                a pírate ship
a sýndicated cólumnist                a Presidéntial eléction

The prísoner was condémned to déath.
The Président resígned from óffice.
After the lécture he was bombárded with quéstions.

### 2  — Read and Look Up —

1. Arnold lacked practical experience in driving a truck.
2. Medical opinion was divided in his case.
3. He didn't have to submit a resignation.
4. His presence in the department would be missed by Lurch.
5. Lurch seemed critical of Arnold's failure to finish the paper.
6. There was no factual evidence that Arnold withdrew from school for medical reasons.
7. Lurch claimed he did not want to publicize the scandal.
8. Dick promised to give his undivided attention to academic work in the future.
9. Lurch remained unaware of Arnold's piracy of books and journals.
10. A hopeless romantic himself, Lurch had little criticism of Arnold for abandoning his academic career.

## III  Intonation

### 1  — Review: Repetition —

| Questions | Answers |
|---|---|
| 1. Are you sensitive to criticism? | I don't like being bombarded with it. |
| 2. Did you get the President's signature? | No, he refused to sign. |
| 3. What makes a neighborhood "residential"? | I think that means the President lives there. |
| 4. Why are you so critical of the government? | I have a right to be indignant, haven't I? |
| 5. You mean they were condemned to death for stealing a boat? | That's the penalty for piracy, you know. |

2 — Practice —

Re-state the following sentences, using your own words. Use another form of the underlined word in each. Use as many (or as few) words as you need.

Examples:

T   He's in *politics*.              S   He's a politician.
    There was an *explosion* in the       A bomb exploded in the hotel.
    hotel.

1. *Political* men are always much distrusted.
2. She made the *suggestion* that we buy tickets early.
3. *Political* affairs are of interest to many students.
4. She writes a *column* for a local newpaper.
5. They made a record of the meeting available to the *public.*
6. He neglected to ask for Arnold's *signature* on the check.
7. They claimed to be interested only in *factual* information.
8. He was a practicing physician for years before he returned to school to take a degree in *physics.*
9. Because of his practical knowledge of *electricity* he was able to repair most home appliances himself.
10. His literary work was definitely in the *Romantic* tradition.
11. You can accuse Arnold of *lunacy,* but that does not mean he could not become a successful *academician.*
12. Because of their *complacency* audiences failed to provide the needed *criticism* of theatrical performances at the universtiy.

3 — Dialog —

Listen to the following dialog and answer the questions at the end.

Final Confrontations

Bob:  What are you doing here today? The term's over.

Dick:  I have a little catastrophe to take care of. Lurch called me in to talk about the paper I did for him.

Bob:  Uh-oh. That sounds catastrophic, all right. My advice is run for your life. Go home
5        and hide under the covers.

Dick:  Catastrophe number two is that I don't have a home. My in-laws have occupied it. And they *know* everything. I have to face them today too—after I face Lurch.

Bob:  Don't you have any *good* news?

Dick:  I can't think of any. I even forgot to bring my lunch today, and I lost my bus
10       fare home.

Bob:  What are a few temporary setbacks? Cheer up. You can always count on your old friends. I'll even treat you to lunch today.

Dick:  Thanks, Bob. That must be the kindest thing you've ever done. I feel better already.

15   Bob:  That's the spirit. Now . . . Oops, I think I see Dr. Lunatic himself coming this way. If you'll excuse me I'll just step out the back.

Dick:  I thought my "old friend" Bob was going to stay and provide moral support.

Bob:  I suggest that you face this alone, Dick. Adversity will temper your spirit. See you at lunch.

20   Dick:  OK. And thanks for all your *help.*

Bob:  Any time.

Dick:  Good morning, Dr. Lurchmint. Did you want to see me?

Dr. Lurchmint:  Yes, indeed. There's something I want to talk to you about.

Dick:  My paper?

25   Dr. Lurchmint:  Well, that's part of it. You did a rather good job, you know.

Dick:  I did?

Dr. Lurchmint:  It was a rather difficult topic. And some of your colleagues failed to
     submit papers at all. But I'm sure you're familiar with the lastest scandal.

Dick:  What scandal?

30   Dr. Lurchmint:  Oh? Well, perhaps I shouldn't have mentioned it at all. I don't care to be
     one who spreads rumors.

Dick:  I'm sure no one would accuse you of indiscretion, Professor.

Dr. Lurchmint:  No, I suppose not. In any case it's bound to become public knowledge
     sooner or later. Well, in short, a certain someone, or rather two certain someones, to
35   be precise, have decided to resign as it were, from the program.

Dick:  Who?

Dr. Lurchmint:  You really don't know? Arnold, of course. He's run off to New York to
     study music with that Tosca fellow. Really without precedent in our department. And
     most distressing of all, he hasn't run off alone.

40   Dick:  What?

Dr. Lurchmint:  You'll never guess who went with him.

Dick:  His mother?

Dr. Lurchmint:  No. Patricia Bevierre.

Dick:  No.

45   Dr. Lurchmint:  Yes.

Dick:  I'm speechless.

Dr. Lurchmint:  So was I, of course. But all this is rather good news for you. That's why
     I called you in. I need a research assistant for next term and, of all those who remain
     with us, you are the best qualified.

50   Dick:  This *is* good news. And at a good time.

Dr. Lurchmint:  Naturally I'll have to discuss the job with you in detail. But that can
     wait till next term. You would appreciate a little vacation, I suppose.

Dick:  Well, I do have a few things to take care of at home.

Dr. Lurchmint:  Certainly. Of course if you get bored in the next few days, you might
55   stop by for a few minutes. Perhaps even, say, tommorrow—if you're not too busy,
     that is.

Dick:  No. Tomorrow I won't be too busy, I guess.

Dr. Lurchmint:  Excellent. We'll just have a little informal chat.

Dick:  Of course, I'll be happy to stop by.

60   Dr. Lurchmint:  Till tommorrow then? Shall we say eight o'clock—sharp?


Questions:

1. Does Dick mean it when he says to Bob "And thanks for all your *help*"?
2. What does Dr. Lurchmint mean when he says "Oh"? to Dick's question?
3. Would you accuse Dr. Lurchmint of indiscretion? Explain.
4. Will Dick have a very restful vacation? Explain.

# LESSON THIRTY — Review —

1 — Review of Sounds: Repetition —

| /i/ | /iy/ |  | /e/ | /ey/ |
|-----|------|--|-----|------|
| sit | seat |  | sell | sale |
| sick | seek |  | debt | date |
| still | steal |  | get | gate |
| will | we'll |  | test | taste |
| his | he's |  | fell | fail |
| it | eat |  | wet | wait |

| /u/ | /uw/ |  | /l/ | /r/ |
|-----|------|--|-----|-----|
| full | fool |  | late | rate |
| pull | pool |  | glass | grass |
| should | shooed |  | collect | correct |
| could | cooed |  | stole | store |

2 — Practice —

Listen to the following sentences. If the word you hear in the blank has the sound of the first word, say 1; if it has the sound of the second word, say 2.

          1   2

1. There's nothing to *(it)* *(eat)*.
2. I *(still)* *(steal)* like my brother.
3. We tried to *(hit)* *(heat)* it.
4. Who's been *(telling)* *(tailing)* you?
5. What kind of *(test)* *(taste)* did they have?
6. I really don't care if they *(fell)* *(fail)*.
7. She gave us the *(long)* *(wrong)* one.
8. *(Collect)* *(Correct)* these papers please.
9. Don't just throw your old papers into the *(file)* *(fire)*.
10. He liked to walk barefoot on the *(glass)* *(grass)*.

## II  Question Tags

1 — Rising Intonation: Repetition —

*Note:* Question tags with rising intonation are used to ask for real information.

117

Questions                                              Answers

1. You have food to eat, don't you?            None. We're out of everything.
2. They tried to hit the target, didn't they?  Yes, but they missed every time.
3. The police aren't still tailing you, are they?   No, I shook them off.
4. We didn't fail the test, did we?            I'm sorry, but you missed every question.
5. He's not still waiting for his brother, is he?   No, now he's waiting for his girlfriend.


2  —  Falling Intonation  —

---

*Note:* Question tags with falling intonation indicate that the speaker does not want new information but expects the listener to agree.

---

Questions                                              Answers

1. You forgot to correct the paragraph, didn't you?   Yes, but I'll do it tonight.

2. He'll fall asleep during the exam, won't he?   Yes, he always does.
3. She hasn't rewritten the article yet,          No, she says she doesn't want to.
   has she?
4. None of them would help you fix the flat       No, they said they were too busy.
   tire, would they?
5. You're leaving town again, aren't you?         Yeah, but I'll be back in a week or two.


3  —  Question and Evasion (Excuse)  —

---

*Note:* Remember that question tags with falling intonation may compel the
listener to agree with something he doesn't like. If so he may *disagree* and
give a reason for his disagreement.

---

Examples:

   T     fail tests            S1   You always fail English tests, don't you?
                               S2   No, I pass some of them.
         play poker            S3   You were up all night playing poker again,
                                    weren't you?
                               S4   No, I was up all night writing my paper.


1.  stay out late                  7.   never save any money
2.  drink too much bourbon         8.   always forget your keys
3.  never eat breakfast            9.   going out to the bar again
4.  chase women (men)             10.   not write home
5.  waste time                    11.   put whiskey in your coffee
6.  eat candy                     12.   not send in application on time

**III   Emphasis and Intonation**

1   —   Special Emphasis (Falling Intonation)   —

---

*Note:* When special emphasis is applied to a word in a sentence with falling intonation, the intonation falls at the point of special emphasis.

Example:

You're taking your mother to the hospital for the opera\tion, aren't /you?

    a.    Special emphasis on *hospital*:

You're taking your mother to the *hos*|pital for the operation, aren't /you?

    b.    Special emphasis on *mother*:

You're taking your *mo*|ther to the hospital for the operation, aren't /you?

---

Example:

He didn't take his dog to the dentist for a check\-up, did /he?

| T   *dentist* | S1   He didn't take his dog to the *den*\tist for a check-up, did /he? |
| | S2   No! He took his dog to a veterinar\ian. |
| T   *dog* | S2   He didn't take his *dog*\ to the dentist for a check-up, did /he? |
| | S3   No! He took his gold\fish to the dentist. |

1.    He didn't study biology as his major fie\ld, did /he?

    T   *major*

        *biology*

2.    You're not buying your son a new car for his birth\day, are /you?

    T   *car*

        *new*

        *son*

3.    She didn't ever fail a written\exam, did /she?

    T   *ever*

        *she*

4.    You didn't eat all those sandwiches for lun\ch, did /you?

    T   *sandwiches*

        *all*

2   —   Special Emphasis (Rising Intonation)   —

---

*Note:* When special emphasis is applied to a word in a sentence with rising intonation, the intonation rises at the point of special emphasis. Example:

Did the boss give you a bonus before the holid/ays?

    a.    Special emphasis on *before*:

Did the boss give you a bonus be/fore the holidays?

    b.    Special emphasis on *you*:

Did the boss give yo/u a bonus before the holidays?

---

Listen and repeat the following sentences. If you are given the cue word, apply special emphasis to that word. If you answer the question, deny the point that is emphasized.

Example:

Are you taking the biology course this seme͞ster?

| T | *this* | S1 | Are you taking the biology course *this͞* semester? |
| | | S2 | No. (I'm taking it next semester.) |
| T | *biology* | S2 | Are you taking the *bio͞logy* course this semester? |
| | | S3 | No. (I'm taking botany.) |
| T | *you* | S3 | Are *yo͞u* taking the biology course this semester? |
| | | S4 | No, not me. (I'm not even a student here.) |

1.  Has he taken all the pictures that he ne͞eds?
    T    *pictures*
    T    *all*
2.  Do you mean some of the textbooks are not available this͞ term?
    T    *textbooks*
    T    *some*
3.  Do you want to play basketball with our school this͞ year?
    T    *our*
    T    *basketball*
4.  Did you say that most of the new students weren't happy with the͞ir schedules?
    T    *weren't*
    T    *new*
    T    *most*

3  —  Double Emphasis / Falling Intonation  —

Examples:

| T | gorilla / apartment | S1 | You can't keep a *gori͞lla* in your *apart͞ment,* can you? |
| | | S2 | No, I'm going to keep *goldfish* in my apartment. |
| | lemons / cereal | S2 | You don't put *le͞mons* in your *cere͞al,* do you? |
| | | S3 | No, I put *bananas* in my cereal. |

beer / soup
ink / hair
car / bedroom
broken glass / driveway
salt / coffee
gloves / feet
hamburger / Chinese restaurant
chair / bathtub
gasoline / swimming pool
shortening / toothbrush

4  —  Double Emphasis / Rising Intonation  —

Examples:
T     onions / bathtub

S1     You have _on⌐ions_ in your _bath⌐tub?_
S2     No, the onions are in the _closet._ I have
       _potatoes_ in the bathtub.

telephone / shower

S2     You have a _tele⌐phone_ in the _sho⌐wer?_
S3     No, the telephone is in the _garbage can._
       The _TV_ is in the shower.

motor oil / salad
bleach / vodka
toothpaste / coffee
money / garbage can
gin / bathtub
shampoo / swimming pool
television / garage
peanut butter / tea

1  —  Affixation No Stress Change: Repetition  —

| | | | |
|---|---|---|---|
| happy | happiness | attend | attendance |
| adult | adulthood | encourage | encouragement |
| friend | friendship | operate | operator |
| rapid | rapidly | profit | profitable |

2  —  Stress Shift Only: Repetition  —

| | | | | | |
|---|---|---|---|---|---|
| stúpid | stupídity | biólogy | biológical | imágine | imaginátion |
| áctive | actívity | áccident | accidéntal | éducate | educátion |

3  —  Vowel Change Only: Repetition  —

| /ey/ | / æ / | /u/ | / ə / | /iy/ | /e/ |
|---|---|---|---|---|---|
| vain | vanity | assume | assumption | brief | brevity |
| nation | national | resume | resumption | deep | depth |

| /ow/ | / ə / | /ay/ | /i/ |
|---|---|---|---|
| phone | phonic | wise | wisdom |
| evoke | evocative | divide | division |

4 — Consonant Change Only: Repetition —

|  /t/  |  /s/  |
|-------|-------|
| pirate | piracy |
| lunatic | lunacy |

|  /k/  |  /s/  |
|-------|-------|
| medical | medicine |
| critical | criticism |
| practical | practice |

| /t/ | /č/ | /d/ | /ž/ |
|-----|-----|-----|-----|
| muscle muscular | fact factual | explode explosion |
| column columnist | suggest suggestion | |

5 — Vowel Change and Stress Shift: Repetition —

| revéal | revelátion | hóstile | hostílity |
|--------|-----------|---------|-----------|
| sýmpathy | sympathétic | réalize | realizátion |

6 — Stress Shift and Consonant Change: Repetition —

| médical | medícinal | pólitics | politícian |
|---------|-----------|----------|-----------|
| públic | publícity | músic | musícian |

7 — Practice —

Restate the following sentences using your own words. Use another form of the underlined word in each. Use as many (or as few) words as you find necessary.

Examples:

| *Regular attendance* is required. | S1 | You have to attend regularly. |
| I admire those people who have the ability to make *music.* | S2 | I admire musicians. |

1. His *hostility* to education revealed a lack of wisdom.
2. *Piracy* is not a profitable activity in the modern world.
3. Her lack of imagination was regarded as *stupidity.*
4. The *encouragement* to enter politics came from his parents.
5. Speeches *critical* of government policies were never made known to the *public.*
6. The *assumption* that friendships are indivisible is false.
7. The President showed little *sympathy* for the rebels' claim to national independence.

this exercise continued on next page

8. The *division* of his wealth among relatives followed immediately after the funeral.
9. *Criticism* of politicians can be *profitable*.
10. *Wisdom* does not necessarily follow on the attainment of *adulthood*.


## V    Intonation

1  —  Practice: Question Words  —

---

*Note:* The ordinary falling intonation on question words indicates that the speaker is requesting information. A rising intonation indicates surprise or a desire for repetition and further explanation.

---

Examples:

| | | |
|---|---|---|
| where / go on vacation (Guam) | S1 | Guess where I'm going on vacation? |
| | S2 | Wh\ere? |
| | S1 | Guam. |
| | S2 | Wh⌐ere? |
| | S1 | Guam. It's a nice little island. |
| when / have dinner | S2 | Guess when we're having dinner. |
| | S3 | Wh⌐en? |
| | S2 | 11:00 o'clock. |
| | S3 | Wh⌐en? |
| | S2 | 11:00 this evening. We're going to a movie first. |

where / have lunch (the White House)
who / come to dinner (Marlon Brando)
when / leave for Europe (in ten minutes)
how / lose so much weight (by eating candy)
what / buy for birthday gift (a rhinoceros)
when / graduate (this afternoon)
who / on TV today (me)
where / get a job (Tahiti)


2  —  Practice: Interrogation  —
Select one student whom you arrest. Question him to determine if he is guilty of drinking while driving a car. Try to use Yes / No questions and question tags with falling intonation. The student arrested should DENY EVERYTHING.
    Example questions:

| | | |
|---|---|---|
| Were you on your way home from a party? | S1 | Well, yes, but . . . |
| Did you stop at the bar downtown? | S1 | No. What bar? |
| Did you have a couple of drinks at home before you left? | S1 | Gosh, no. |
| You had quite a few, didn't you? | S1 | No, none at all. |

Other suggested "crimes":

1. spitting on the sidewalk
2. cheating on a test
3. selling LSD to classmates
4. leaving a restaurant without paying the bill
5. stealing library books